The Perversion of Science

An Attack on God and Man

© by Tom Volinchak

CONTENTS

Introduction
    The Perversion of Science i

Chapter One
    The Basic Science Toolbox 1

Chapter Two
    Theories, Laws, Observations, and the Universal Language of Science 26

Chapter Three
    Clean, Renewable, Sustainable Energy 35

Chapter Four
    Anthropogenic Climate Change – Global Warming 74

Chapter Five
    Big Bang Theory and Creationism 97

Chapter Six
    NASA: A Real Global Threat. 111

Chapter Seven
    Water, Precious Water. 131

Chapter Eight
    Oil, Precious Oil 148

Chapter Nine
    Little Green Men 160

Chapter Ten
    Indestructible Earth 171

Chapter Eleven
    Evolution 187

Chapter Twelve
   Carbon Dating and the Age of Earth. 191
Chapter Thirteen
   Sustainability 196
Chapter Fourteen
   Parting Thoughts. 202

About the Author 205

INTRODUCTION

The Perversion of Science

It is hard to think of any aspect of our daily lives in which we are not bombarded with scientific information. In the '60s when I was a boy, news about science was pretty much limited to the space program and the latest medical discoveries.

Today, however, at every turn we experience scientific news about cell phones, computers, vitamins, automobiles, light bulbs, bed mattresses, shoes and even hair gel. Fortunately, most of this stuff is innocuous and we have become pretty good at quickly sifting through it.

What is not so easy to ignore, however, and what has become quite troubling are the ever-repetitive claims about the impending demise of the earth, complete with depletion of our resources and literally the end of life as we know it.

Alarmingly, this new wave of scientific information is being weaved into the fabric of our society. Some of this information is easy to spot. For instance, God promises us an indestructible planet, endless abundance, a stable universe, and clearly defined genders.[1] But the "experts" tell us otherwise, insisting that these matters can only be guided and controlled by man.

Some of the misinformation, however, is much more insidious,

1	Psalm 37:29, Psalm 104:5, Ecclesiastes 1:4, Isaiah 45:18, Revelation 11:18 Matthew 19:28, Luke 23:43, Matthew 6:26, Matthew 6:28-30.

because disguised as helpful policy, it is aimed at controlling our religious freedoms, educational choices, and constitutional rights.

At the hands of elected officials, corporations, entertainers, and sports figures, scientific claims and information are being delivered in a manner that in my opinion, chips away at the very tenets of Christianity, and is drawing multitudes away from our Savior and God the Father.

I do not believe that this is a simple, random, secular trend that is characteristic of the times. I believe instead that it is well orchestrated and managed by Satan, employing his minions, and many unwitting, ignorant, self-drunk average citizens who already deny God. This is a vicious war against everything that is good and wholesome.

Decades ago, sexual perversion, greed, and ego were the swords by which Satan decimated Christians. Today, however, he employs far more destructive weapons in the form of what I have branded as perverted science.

As you read my book you will find that I am not by any means a theologian or a highly astute biblical scholar. Like you, I am a student of the Bible, but not one who readily commands every applicable scripture that might apply to the points and arguments I am making. I am, however, a Christian anchored so firmly that I recognize the vicious attack being carried out against us disguised as science.

As a Christian, I have endured countless peer attacks, loss of opportunities and promotions, public ridicule, and insults because I have dared to speak of God in the same breath as Einstein, Gauss and Boyle. I would bet dollars to doughnuts that you too have suffered these very same things in your own attempts to advise that

Scripture explains what man often cannot.

Make no mistake, when we walk with those who claim to be saving the planet, finding life in space, and discovering true sustainability, we are walking away from Jesus Christ, his Father, and all that has been promised to us.

As a man of science, I have never found a single example in which Scripture and Christianity contradicted any lesson, principle, law, reaction, force, behavior, theory, or other aspect of science.

I wrote *The Perversion of Science* to help us come to a better understanding of our life on earth. As you read, you will repeatedly find me referring to misleading scientific information as perversion, and the individuals spreading this malfeasance as perversionists.

If we are being honest, we must admit that as a nation, our general understanding of mathematics and science is lacking. This lack of education is a deadly chink in our armor that allows the perversionist to attack us with misleading science. My book is intended to be a sword to sever these deceptions from the reality that God blessed us with.

Most readers of this book will already have a strong grip on Scripture and God's message to us. The challenge, however, is that the pagan, the doubter, the non-believer believes that science trumps Scripture, and they often classify the word as fairy tales. As soon as we inject God into a conversation with non-believers, they scoff, turn their ear, and run.

I did not write this book to say Scripture is lacking in the ability to attract lost souls, but instead to fortify and demonstrate that science and Scripture are in concert. I wrote this book to demonstrate that science is not a secular discipline; it is 100 percent born of God.

My promise to you is that using this book as a tool, there is no environmentalist, no academic expert or anyone else who will be able to hold ground with us and denigrate God's promises using manipulated, partial, and perverted science.

The Perversion of Science will reach out to you differently than other books written under God's hand. As a necessity to achieve our goal, the first two chapters are very technical and will be presented in the form of classroom lessons. I promise, however, if you patiently proceed through these chapters, you will emerge far better prepared to shoot down the perversionist. Even more importantly, you will be able to illuminate to him that God and science are in concert. It is by this process that we will squash this new, vicious attack on our faith.

Understand also that it is not necessary to develop an instant command of the scientific principles shared in the first two chapters. This information is something you can come back to for reference and fortification any time you feel God's promise of a perfect planet is being attacked.

Recruiting others into the realm of God has never been more important. Unfortunately, the digital world in which we live makes this extremely difficult.

While Scripture gives us the direction with which to lead people, it is our blessings of worldly skills and talents that provide the tools required to capture the attention of the secular world.

Among my own blessings is a command of science. My most passionate desire is that the fruits of my life's work, this book, will help you stand against those who pervert science and use it to attack God and his promises to us.

Enjoy!

Chapter One

The Basic Science Toolbox

We have all heard that Americans trail other leading industrialized nations when it comes to science and mathematics. I don't know if this is true, but in general I do know that most people don't really have a strong drive to undertake comprehensive studies of these topics.

However, to prevent having our faith attacked by scientific perversion, it is important that we have a basic technical foundation at our disposal. As such, I am pleased to present you with something I call the *Basic Science Toolbox*.

This toolbox is a concise collection of some of the most powerful laws, principles and fundamentals of science and offers a common and universal starting point for all scientific discoveries. Any scientific claim or discovery that ignores these tools must be considered science fiction.

These tools won't make you a science expert, but they will give you an unshakeable foundation by which you can better understand, critique, and demolish the scientific attacks being levied toward Christianity. A command of these tools will allow you to stand firmly in the face of any scientist or questionable scientific claim and then force a debate based only on truth. In more complex issues, having these basic tools at your fingertips will allow you to enhance your personal journey with science. Upon the completion of this chapter on science and math basics, you will be armed to join me in future chapters as we discuss climate change, little green men, and the spontaneous origin of man.

While there is Scripture cited in this chapter, later chapters will highlight passages from the Bible that will allow science to glow in the warmth and wisdom of God's word. It is important that we come to a better understanding of the science that is part of God's blessings to us. I believe this is both a worldly and a Christian responsibility that we cannot ignore.

Without further delay, and in no specific order of importance, here are the tools everyone should have at hand when discussing scientific matters.

The first law of thermodynamics

This law is commonly called the law of conservation of energy. It tells us that in nature, on our planet, energy cannot be created or destroyed. It tells us that energy is a constant that cannot and does not fluctuate. It tells us that the exact amount of energy that was available when the earth was created is the same amount of energy that is available now.[2]

In spiritual terms it tells us that what God created, man cannot destroy. It points out that God created energy![3]

Let's take a look at this important law represented as a simple, easy-to-understand equation.

Potential energy (PE) = kinetic energy (KE)

A simple visualization of this is to imagine a ball sitting on a six-foot-high ledge. This ball has a certain potential energy that will

---

[2] https://www.sciencedirect.com/topics/chemistry/first-law-of-thermodynamics.
[3] https://blogs.timesofisrael.com/energy-is-evidence-of-god/, Genesis 1:1.

only be discharged when the ball is rolled off the shelf edge. If you have ever sensed the danger of standing at the edge of a very high place and fretting about what would happen if you stepped off, then you have experienced the property of potential energy. Once our ball is pushed off the shelf, the force of what we call gravity begins pulling the ball downward, converting the now-diminishing potential energy into another form that is called kinetic energy. Kinetic energy is commonly known as the energy of motion. An important observation to make here is that as the ball falls, it loses potential energy but gains speed, and accordingly kinetic energy.

Where this law defends Scripture is in arguments where someone maintains that God's earth is running out of energy, or that some new technology is more energy efficient than another. Make no mistake, some machines are more efficient than others in the amount of work they can do per energy unit consumed, but none of these new technologies can save or destroy energy.

Let us now expand this general equation into the accepted academic equation taught universally in every physics class.

$(m)(g)(h) = \frac{1}{2}(m)(v^2)$

m = the weight of the object in kilograms

g = the fixed constant of acceleration due to gravity (9.8 m/sec-sec)

h = the height the ball is being held

v = the velocity in meters-per-second that the object is traveling

Here is one important value of this equation: If you knew for instance how high the object was being held, you could solve the equation to determine how fast the object would be going at various points along its fall. The beauty of this basic equation is that it demonstrates again this infallible law of nature: *Energy cannot be created or destroyed.* It can only be converted into other forms of energy.

So, the earth is running out of energy? So, man must create new, clean forms of energy? God says otherwise, and now you can see, so does science.

In the deeper disciplines of science, this equation is expanded to include many different types of energy consumption and is not limited to just the force of gravity. For instance, a conservation equation might take the form of calculating the potential energy of a gallon of gasoline and determining how much work it will do when burned in a combustion engine. That equation simplified might look something like this:

$$ce = (w) + (\Delta)$$

ce = the total potential combustion energy of the gallon of fuel

w = the total amount of work expressed in horsepower per hour

Δ = energy that winds up being converted to heat

Another important aspect we must understand about energy is further demonstrated by these equations. Once the activity is completed, in this case the gasoline burning, there will still be the same amount of energy available as there was before the action took place. A new conservation equation will prove how this works.

Imagine the gasoline was burned in an engine and the horsepower generated was used by a crane to lift furniture up to a third-floor apartment. The new conservation equation would look something like this:

$$w = (m)(g)(h) + \Delta$$

w = the total amount of work expressed in horsepower – hours
m = the weight of the furniture
g = the fixed constant of acceleration due to gravity (9.8 m/sec-sec)
h = the height the furniture is now resting at
Δ = heat lost due to combustion

In this case it is interesting to note that work done by the engine can be translated into the terms of potential energy plus heat just as described in our first equation.

The casual observer might maintain that energy is not conserved, because once heat is produced, it is lost to the environment. Such is not the case, and it is important for us to understand why. The energy converted to heat will indeed be absorbed into the environment but then it will be further converted into different and new forms of energy. For instance, some of the heat might be used by plants to grow and produce carbohydrates by way of photosynthesis. That plant energy would then be converted perhaps to muscle action by the person who consumed the plant; on and on it goes. Some of the heat might also be consumed by natural biochemical processes that over time produce coal, oil or even diamonds.

What we must remember again is that no matter which process we might be considering, energy is always conserved. All consumptions of energy result in the creation of an equal amount of work, heat and waste; that is to say, other forms of energy.

The real takeaway here is that when someone speaks to us about a renewable or clean energy, they are indeed speaking perverted science because all energy use creates waste, and all energy is conserved, therefore renewable. God already made energy renewable.

The only thing man can do with energy is to convert it into different forms.

Many times, when we read Scripture, we often fail to understand just how broad and all-encompassing God's promises to us are. The following wisdom is just one example.

<u>Matthew 6:26 NIV</u>

Look at the birds of the air, they do not sow or reap or stow away in barns and yet your heavenly Father feeds them. Are you not much more valuable than they?

We can clearly see that *Matthew 6:26* applies to God making sure we have more than just the obvious necessities. It applies to energy as well.

When God advised us not to fear for our daily needs, you can bet the law of conservation of energy was a gift he gave us along with his assurance.

<u>The law of conservation of matter</u>

Proven generations ago, this law states that in a closed system such as our planet, matter can neither be created nor destroyed. In all chemical, physical, and radioactive events, just as we have learned with energy, the matter found at the beginning of an event will be equal to the matter after the event.

A very interesting issue to keep in your hip pocket is that it isn't just the amount of matter that is constant, but also the individual type of matter. So, in essence, the same amount of copper or manganese that was present at the dawn of earth is indeed the same amount of that material on earth today.[4]

A chemical representation of the conservation of matter can be demonstrated by adding hydrochloric acid to sodium hydroxide. When combined, the two chemicals produce water, salt and heat.

This equation can be represented as

$HCl + NaOH \Leftrightarrow H_2O + NaCl + \Delta$ (heat)

The equation demonstrates that the amounts of sodium, hydrogen, oxygen, chloride, and energy are the same before, after and during the chemical reaction. The compounds change, but the individual ingredient amounts do not.

The law of conservation of mass holds true for every activity of mankind, and as with the conservation of energy, man can convert mass into different forms, but he cannot create or destroy the basic components of it.

Take the example of a burning piece of paper. One might believe that the act of burning the paper does destroy mass. Since the paper vanishes when we burn it, doesn't that prove that all the mass simply went up in smoke? No, this is not what it proves. By using proper laboratory instrumentation, we can prove that the paper was merely converted into an equal weight of gasses, metals, water, and ash material.

Adding insult to injury for those who attack Christianity with perverted science, we see that *Matthew 6:26* also applies to God making sure we always have the required materials for sustaining life. Man cannot destroy a single physical thing God created. Not

---

4   https://chem.libretexts.org/Bookshelves/Introductory_Chemistry/The_Basics_of_GOB_Chemistry_(Ball_et_al.)/05%3A_Introduction_to_Chemical_Reactions/5.01%3A_The_Law_of_Conservation_of_Matter.

through nuclear explosion, particle accelerator, spaceship, weapon, or chemistry has man ever destroyed even the smallest amount of matter.

Perversionist self-contradiction alert – an amusing detour

I am likely to repeat the following narrative later in the book, as I write it, but I want to share with you a formative and foundational mainstay of my message.

The attack on God using science is nothing new and it has been happening, right under our noses, for decades, even centuries. Quite often scientists reach a dead end when trying to prove their theories, and rather than admit their failure, more often than not, at the risk of losing their funding, book sales, or stature in the scientific community, they reinvent their message to create counterfeit science, which enables them to continue their work.

Many times, these works may strike us as small, harmless, parochial studies that do not seem to hold broad implications for us, but many times these scientists, without realizing it, are purposely driven by their hate for God and their work serves as just another fortification on the attack of which I speak. Many times, these perversions slip under our radar. For these reasons we must become more vigilant and scientifically attentive.

Albert Einstein's $E=mc^2$ is a foundational platform of science and should be considered as genius. Even at that, unlike Scripture, it has holes in it. We must accept that this discovery, within boundaries, holds up to the test of scientific genius.

Where Einstein fell into perversion, however, is that he maintained that matter could be created from energy.[5]

I am firm in believing that this proclamation was a seed planted

5   https://plato.stanford.edu/entries/equivME/.

The Perversion of Science

with the sole purpose of suggesting that God did not create all things, but that all things came from nothing.[6] For decades this nonsense has been a part of scientific education. Many scientists not only believe this, but have dedicated their lives proving it. Let us examine how this is going on today.

To support these types of mass creation claims, scientists have documented that in certain subatomic collisions/reactions the total mass measured after a new particle was formed was less than the individual mass of the two particles before the collision. The scientist maintained that because of this observed loss of mass, their quantum mechanics proves both an exception to the law of mass conservation, and that man can indeed create and destroy matter. They believe they have proved that the universe did not require God to create, but instead was formed by a random event known as the big bang.

Once again, however, Scripture prevailed and the perversionist's nonsense started to collapse on itself.

From my earliest days of college study, I always maintained that the reason scientists often found less mass after certain quantum collisions was that these collisions created new, smaller particles that man simply had not yet developed the technology to detect. I maintained that their findings were simply incomplete and ignorant of the full complexity of Creation.

Well, lo and behold, recent discoveries have proven exactly that. As we should always expect, challenging God and trying to understand his wonder will never end well for the scientist. If I could go to Las Vegas and place bets on God versus research scientists, I would be

---

6   https://www.washingtonpost.com/archive/opinions/1984/06/03/our-universe-created-from-nothing/dc8282d7-ae75-4149-b3c5-49e4614b2f36/.

the richest man in the world.

The following series of events illustrates just how impotent man's ability to understand Creation is.

A Nobel Prize was recently given for the discovery of a heretofore unseen subatomic particle called the Higgs boson particle.[7]

The particle was originally heralded for its potential to reveal the secrets as to why matter has mass, to finally explaining and proving that gravity, and finally proving that like God, man can create and destroy matter.

To the dismay of these perversionists, what the Higgs boson particle demonstrated was that God's Creation is composed of many smaller particles whose existence science was embarrassingly unaware of. It also foretells that there are more, even smaller particles than the ones we do not yet have the technology to find. Just when they thought they were God, they got smacked down by him.

Here is the hilarious part of this particle discovery. As the Higgs boson particle has now exposed just how little man knows about mass and matter, essentially God's Creation, these frustrated quantum scientists have unwittingly fallen on bended knee before the Almighty. In the failed humiliation of trying to define Creation, the Higgs boson particle has been nicknamed, get ready for it, "the God Particle."[8]

How magnificent is God? Even those who despise him, who research to prove he doesn't exist, wind up using his name to

---

7   https://home.cern/science/physics/higgs-boson.
8   https://www.aspenideas.org/sessions/the-god-particle?utm_source=google&utm_medium=adgrant&utm_campaign=-Science&utm_term=the%20god%20particle&gclid=CjwKCAiAksyN-BhAPEiwAlDBeLCQ1MbXpE5PwgUBndUUEB-uxyvNT90WqPx-25eQ5BOMIW0O5BIr69iRoCP4oQAvD_BwE.

explain what they cannot understand. Indeed, every knee shall bow.

I am here to tell you firsthand that there are some life mysteries that are far beyond man's ability to understand. We all must admit that science constantly gives us new understandings of our world; however, science is a gift provided to us by God and no matter how smart we become we will never be able to explain Creation.

We can expect the perversionists to continue his quest to understand and explain Creation, and we can expect that they will continue to fail.

Before I move on let me try to clarify the real-world biblical importance of the Higgs boson discovery and how it applies to believers and non-believers alike.

Those who built the Tower of Babel sought to get physically closer to God. The lessons taught in this story are crucial to us living in accordance with God's wishes.

Be attentive to this lesson for I maintain that the frustrations scientists experienced with the discovery of the Higgs boson particle are parallel to the frustrations experienced by the builders of the Tower of Babel. God was displeased and he put an end to the foolishness by causing workers to suddenly speak in different tongues, thereby leaving the project in total confusion.

The Higgs dead end is perhaps a much milder warning, but only a fool ignores hints and warnings from God and then continues to mock him. I shudder to think about what an angered God could bring upon one of the mega-powered atom smashers if he decided he had enough of this blasphemous search for the secrets of Creation.

<u>Hebrews 11:3</u>

By faith we understand that the universe was created by the word of God, so that what is seen was not made out of things that are visible.

<u>The second law of thermodynamics</u>

This indefatigable law has to do with the phenomenon called entropy, or maximum disorder. In simple terms it tells us that the energy of any system will seek to reach equilibrium, or in other words, find a resting state.[9]

A common demonstration of this can be carried out by holding a jar of marbles upside down with a hand keeping the marbles from falling out. While the hand is holding the marbles back, we now understand that the suspended marbles have potential energy. However, once the hand is pulled away, the marbles will fall to the ground, bounce, roll, and spread out (kinetic energy) until each marble has come to a complete stop. When all the marbles have stopped, the system has discharged all of its energy, and no further movement is possible. At this point it is said that the marbles have reached equilibrium.

Before I continue, it must be noted that there is an additional vital component of this law and that is the principle of randomness. It states that no matter how many times an experiment or natural release of energy is repeated, a different maximum disorder configuration will be achieved. In the case of the marbles, each time they are dropped, they will come to rest in a unique, never to be duplicated, random scattering.

The second law of thermodynamics also teaches us that random events will never produce orderly outcomes.

---

9   https://www.livescience.com/50941-second-law-thermodynamics.html.

No matter how many times one releases the marbles, they will never come to rest forming an image of Babe Ruth; they will never settle into groups arranged uniformly by color or size, and they will never form a single-file line. The result will always be a unique random event of maximum disorder.

When someone suggests that Creation happened from a random event, now you see that such an idiotic claim not only insults God, but science as well.

The law of equilibrium

This is another fundamental law in biology, chemistry, and physics. A law that rules all physical events, this is perhaps the most neglected and conveniently omitted principle of those who pervert science. When forced to obey this law, many modern-day concepts believed to be scientific fall apart and are rendered to be nothing more than flimflam.

Equilibrium, a key player in the second law of thermodynamics essentially tells us that for any physical, chemical, astronomical, or radioactive event, the event will always come to rest in the exact same state.[10] It is the state in which energy on both sides of the event or reaction is equal. There is no such thing as perpetual motion. All natural events come to rest. The following example will help to illustrate.

Imagine two clear five-gallon containers that are connected near their base by a clear plastic tube. Now imagine that the clear plastic connecting tube has a valve that can either allow or prevent water to pass either way. If the valve is open, water can pass from one container to the other. When the valve is closed, whatever water is in each container stays in that container. If we close the valve and fill one container with four gallons of water, the water remains in

10   https://www.merriam-webster.com/dictionary/equilibrium.

the container and is at equilibrium. Our studies taught us that this water has potential energy and wants to achieve a lower level, but like the ball high on a shelf waiting to be pushed off, the water can go nowhere until the valve is open. The valve, by the way, is exerting the same force back against the water that the water is exerting on the valve. At this point, the valve and the four gallons of water are at equilibrium with each other.

Once we open the valve, water will pass freely from the first container into the second until the water finally levels out, putting two gallons of water in both containers. Both containers now have the same potential energy, but the water will no longer move, even if the valve is left open, because both containers have reached physical equilibrium. No matter how many times you perform this experiment it will never happen that one container winds up with more water than the other. Equilibrium is always reached in nature.

Later, when we dissect the perversionist's attacks on God, we will see that apocalyptic theories generally neglect this principle of science.

Standardized data measurement

For any scientific theory to hold water, the data involved in the analysis must be standardized. Standardized data is that which is gathered in the same exact way, using the same exact measurements, instrumentation, and methods. In a perfect experiment, not only would all the data be standardized, but it would also be homogenous, which is to say, collected in identical conditions.[11]

In the real world, especially with experiments conducted over long periods of time, it is often difficult to have totally standardized data. Good science always documents the possible discrepancies of the various methods used to collect data and then informs the

11   https://www.sisense.com/glossary/data-standardization/.

observer of where the results and conclusions may be suspect. By understanding how data is collected and reported, we can come to more educated conclusions about scientific claims.

To make scientific attacks on Christianity seem reasonable, the perversionist will all too frequently misrepresent, manipulate or even, as in the case of global warming, omit data that doesn't support the desired conclusion. Let's look at how the analysis of numbers can be manipulated to sell us snake oil.

Imagine that two different physicians are being considered to administer a new health-giving medicine to a patient. The drug dose must be determined and administered based on body weight within a very tight specification range. To be extra thorough, the patient decides to see two doctors we will name Doctor Green and Doctor Blue.

At the end of a two-week study, Doctor Green provides a report that states that between his two office locations he recorded the patient's weight five times per day for a total of seventy measurements. The treatment weight of the patient, by his measurements, was found to average 171.3044 pounds. Based on his extensive measurements, Doctor Green prescribes an appropriate dosage.

Meanwhile, Doctor Blue announces that over the same two-week period, he weighed the patient at his office once every day, for a total of fourteen measurements and found the patient to weigh 172.2 pounds. Based on his findings, he suggests a dosage that is more potent than the one being prescribed by his colleague.

Which doctor would you trust to have the better results? The natural tendency would be to choose Doctor Green who did the most exhaustive testing. The truth is that we don't have enough scientific information to make a proper decision. A deeper look into this theoretical example reveals some important details about the numbers that could easily have been overlooked.

As it turned out, Doctor Green weighed the patient at many different times during the day, sometimes before and sometimes after a meal or exercise. He also weighed the patient at two different locations using two different scales.

Conversely, Doctor Blue always weighed the patient at three o'clock in the afternoon, on the same scale in the same location. The result is that even though Doctor Green recorded the most data, there was more variance and potential error in his seventy weight samples than in Doctor Blue's fourteen samples. Doctor Green not only had to calibrate two different instruments but make a calculated guess at the possible differences between the two scales.

Conversely, by using one scale, one location, one technician and a specific time of weighing, Doctor Blue provided results with a higher degree of standardization, and as such, emerges as the more accurate physician.

Perversionists perceive God's world as imperfect, and in their attempt to save it with science, often report findings and observations that violate the scientific requirements of standardized data. It is important that before we buy into a scientific claim, we find out how the associated data was collected.

Significant figures

Intimately intertwined with standardized data is the scientific convention known as significant figures. Significant figures is the convention that enables reputable scientists to describe, document and communicate to others the exact sensitivity and accuracy of their research findings and observations.[12] Because most people do not understand the rules of significant figures, the corruption of this convention is also frequently used as a tool for the unscrupulous scientist to make faulty research look believable to the public. Continuing with our example of two doctors recording patient weights, let's look at how significant figures can be manipulated to promote fraudulent science.

Imagine that Doctor Green used a scale that was accurate within +/- 2 pounds, while Doctor Blue used a digital scale that was accurate to within +/- 0.1, or one-tenth of a pound.

Doctor Green totaled his seventy weight samples and divided them by the number seventy to arrive at his average patient weight of 171.3044 pounds. The untrained observer would accept this methodology and consider the number 171.3044 pounds to be a reliable number. But make no mistake that the number represented by Doctor Green is fraudulent and not scientifically acceptable. Let us see why.

The number 171.3044 indicates a scale accuracy of seven significant figures, or in other words, accuracy to one-ten-thousandth of a pound. We know that Doctor Green's scale was only capable of accuracy +/- 2 pounds, so from the point of view of scientific validity, Doctor Green can only accurately represent his patient's weight within a four-pound range. That is two pounds possible error high plus two pounds possible error low.

Here is why this is so important. Imagine that the required safe medicine dosage had to be accurate within one-fourth of a pound. In that case Doctor Green could not prescribe a proper dose; because his overall margin of error is four pounds, that means he can only say with accuracy that his patient weighs somewhere

---

12   http://www.astro.yale.edu/astro120/SigFig.pdf.

between 169.3044 and 173.3044 pounds. This is ten times more variable than the required accuracy.

Conversely, by having an instrument that is accurate to within +/- 0.1 pound, Doctor Blue's stated patient weight average of 172.2 pounds provides an accurate total maximum weight variance of 172.1–172.3 pounds, a range safely within the required drug prescription range of 0.25 pounds.

Dangerously, all the apocalyptic environmental information being given to the public purposely sidesteps the proper use of significant figures. As you will see a bit later, global temperature readings, carbon dating and evolution theory are among the most blatant and egregious offenders of proper data representation.

Sample size

Another attempt by perversionists to give credibility to bogus research is the convenient manipulation of sample size. Sample size tells us how many observations were made during the scientific claim we are being asked to consider. By itself, a sample size tells us nothing about the accuracy of any study. To have any scientific significance, a study must share with us more than just the sample size but also the total number of possible samples that could have been taken from the entire phenomenon being studied.[13]

For example, if I told you that I took one thousand samples of an event, you might lean toward believing that I performed a thorough study. However, you would call me a charlatan if I then shared with you that those samples were one thousand individual spins on a Las Vegas slot machine and based on my findings I was advising people that they could expect to win if they invested their life savings.

---

13   https://www.ncbi.nlm.nih.gov/pmc/articles/PMC2993974/.

Most people can look at a small-scale study and get a feel as to whether enough data has been gathered to make it credible. In football for instance, predicting how an NFL running back will perform the next year, barring injury, by assessing the past five years of his running data is probably a reasonable line of prediction.

But what if we tried to predict his future performance by only analyzing three of his past games? Chances are high that we wouldn't get an accurate result since in a small sample size of three games, we might pick one day where he was sick, or the weather was bad, or his offensive line was injured, or even a game where he set all-time records. In other words, if we tried to judge him based on only three games, chances are we would capture some very untypical results, and our conclusions would be inaccurate. In this case, our sample size would be too small for our predictions to be accurate.

The misrepresentation of sample size is a typical tool with which scientific perversionists attack Creation, God, and Christianity. Later in the book as we look at the individual scientific claims being made today, we will illuminate actual sample size fraud associated with those claims. For now, the crucial point is that when we analyze any scientific claim, we should begin by first examining how much data was collected compared to the total size of all data that was available.

Comparative numbers

Most people judge numbers based on their own personal life experience, so the perceived size and importance of a number will be different depending on who it is that is reading or analyzing that number. Those who indulge in scientific perversion commonly use large numbers to confuse reality and make their claims look ironclad. However, often, a closer look will expose these seemingly big numbers to be too small to provide scientific validity. Understanding the comparative relationship of numbers in the world of science is tantamount to not being fooled by hoaxes. The following example may seem oversimplified, but it will serve as a starting point.

Try to imagine the impact you would feel if you were to begin a new career that paid a salary of $1 million per year. For most of us, this would be a mega-financial dream come true. However, for a man like Elon Musk, this income level would be a pittance. With his responsibilities and expenses, a million-dollar salary would cause him to file for bankruptcy.

This is the comparative nature of numbers. What is large or small to one person may have a totally different impact on another. We cannot allow ourselves to make value judgments based solely on the impact the researchers' numbers make on us.

In science, there are no big or small numbers; there are simply numbers. In science, numbers serve only to describe and compare results, research, and outcomes. In science, there is no emotional component to a number—there is no "wow factor." In science, numbers only have meaning if we are also given the details of what these numbers are compared against.

In college I undertook an individual research project in which I studied the pH of the local Mahoning River. For my grade, I was required to present a paper containing my findings, observations, and conclusions. To impress my professor, I involved friends and family to collect samples for me at different times and locations along the river. At the end of nine weeks, I had amassed 642 pH samples and was confident that I could put forth some interesting conclusions.

I earned a grade of B, I believe mostly for effort, because in the review of my paper, my professor noted that researchers had been studying the pH of the Mahoning River since the early days of the Industrial Revolution when steel mills first came to my hometown, Youngstown, Ohio. My professor pointed out that my 642 samples taken over nine weeks were minuscule when compared to the hundreds of thousands of samples that had been taken fifty years prior. I learned that while my conclusions based on my 642 observations were indeed sound and sensible, compared to the many events that happened to this river over fifty years, I simply didn't have enough information and sample size for my conclusions to hold water.

This is an example of how even with the best intentions a study can fail both the requirements of comparative numbers and proper sample size.

Isn't it funny how on one hand perversionists want us to believe that the earth is almost fourteen billion years old, but on the other hand, armed with only a few years of unreliable, variable, non-standardized data want people to believe that their anti-Christian, anti-scientific apocalyptic theories are true? One of the best defenses that we can have against those who pervert science is a command of the comparative nature of numbers.

Shallow conclusions

Since the dawn of time, a shallow conclusion has been a powerful and dangerous tool used by immoral scientists to deceive the public and reap the benefits of personal agendas. Shallow conclusion is a tool of those who promote global warming, the big bang, evolution, and the other nonsense that this book will expose to be fraudulent. Shallow conclusions work much the same as the magician's sleight of hand. The magician tells the audience to focus on something and then watch the results. What we know, of course, is that by focusing on what the magician tells us, we miss the magician's manipulation and are left believing that we saw something that defied the laws of nature.

There is a mesmerizing Internet trick floating around in which a charming Internet wizard shows the viewer six face cards. He asks the viewer to focus on only one card and memorize it. He then boasts that by magic he can determine which one of the face cards we chose. After choosing your card the magician gives you his "abracadabra," and takes you to another screen that shows five face cards, and voila, your card is no longer there. How did he do it?

Here is how he did it. He first showed us six face cards and asked us to focus on one. What we didn't realize is that when screen number two popped up it wasn't just the card that we picked that was gone, but all six original face cards were removed. Since all face cards have great similarity, and since the viewer was only focused on one card, very few ever notice that all six cards from the original screen are removed from the second screen. Of course, our card is gone. All the original cards are gone as well so it didn't matter which card we picked.

This is a small example of just how convincing the perversion of shallow conclusion can be, and believe it or not, these types of vaudevillian antics occur at the highest levels of the scientific community. We are attacked by these kinds of tricks with nutrition, health, and financial products every day. Let's take a real-life look at how easily scientists can and do deceive us.

Imagine that researchers observe that 80 percent of people with heart problems eat red meat. As a result, they claim red meat is a cause of heart problems in 80 percent of patients. You might ask, "What is the problem with that?" Here is the problem. If the same researcher studied how many of those same people had flat feet, ear lobes, or perhaps brown hair, he very well might find that 80 percent of people with these characteristics also had heart problems.

So, if a different scientist wanted, if it fit his agenda, he could very well conclude that it was flat feet and not red meat that caused heart problems. So, who is correct?

This is a simple analogy, but it is a sobering example of how data can be manipulated to deliver shallow conclusions and mislead the public.

All too often today we are influenced by scientists who do not want us to see the complete discovery of information. These scoundrels selectively omit information and then maintain that anyone who dares to call for additional information is a crackpot.

Sadly, our government and media support this kind of scientific perversion and help shield the public from knowing all the facts. The lesson to be learned here is that before accepting any scientific claim, especially those suggesting that man must act to correct God's failures, we must demand to see the conflicting views and the complete set of research data. We cannot accept shallow conclusions.

Scientific protocol and empirical evidence

Since the dawn of scientific exploration, in the pure and orthodox disciplines of research and discovery, theorists of opposing views have always engaged a spirited and open rivalry. Scientific protocol has always demanded the equal sharing, discussion, and debate of all new information. Scientific information is meant to be presented publicly, voluminously, and freely without bias.[14] If

---

14   https://www.livescience.com/21456-empirical-evidence-a-definition.html.

you think about it, this makes good sense. No matter how bitter the rivalry of opposing scientific camps might be, in the end, when all discoveries and points of view are presented equally and openly, the public gets to hear the truth so that sound personal judgments can be made.

Furthermore, no honest, rational scientist would ever present new ideas or technologies to the public that had not withstood rigorous testing and critique beforehand. Science depends on, and cannot advance without, opposing views. Time and time again we have lived to see drugs, chemicals, medical discoveries, food, and health issues forced down our throats as the newest wave of modern science, only to find out years later that we would have been a lot better off had we stopped and listened to the voices of dissent. Let us not forget that many of the greatest discoveries of mankind came not from the majority riding the popular bandwagon of the day, but instead from the lone voices of contrary, out-of-the-box thinking.

Back in the day, scientific consensus claimed that Thomas Edison, Christopher Columbus, and the Wright brothers were lunatics. The same so-called scientific consensus assured us that cigarettes, DDT, thalidomide, and asbestos were safe for human exposure. History is bursting with examples of how often scientific consensus is wrong.

This scientific history must raise red flags with us about the potentially fatal consequences of uncontested scientific bandwagons. We can no longer automatically accept the doctrine of individuals like Neil DeGrasse Tyson, Al Gore, Bill Nye and Stephen Hawking. We can no longer provide uncontested stages to those who spread perverted science.

When scientific claims do not readily share all contrary findings, data and theories, we can be certain that those scientific claims are bogus.

What kind of quality discovery fears critique and challenge? What kind of scientist summarily dismisses any thinking that does not agree with his theory? It is deplorable that the American media assists in these practices. Great scientists like Salk and Tesla never tried to squash their detractors. These men set the example of scientific protocol, and we must hold all scientific discoveries to the same standard. If we do not, then scientific truth, our faith, and God's promises to us, will always finish second to the perversionist's personal agenda.

Psalm 106:3

Blessed are they who observe justice, who do righteousness at all times.

Chapter Two

Theories, Laws, Observations, and the Universal Language of Science

As we begin dismantling scientific perversions it will be helpful for us to understand what I call the language of science. The universal language of science is an important guide that enables us to take into proper consideration all observations, theories and laws when making judgments about scientific claims. It is a language that creates transparency for all scientific claims and provides a common protocol for our conversations.

Key clarifications

*form *In this chapter, when I speak of scientific laws, I am expanding the scope to address the laws that prescribe the way scientists are committed to work, interact, behave, and communicate their work to us.*

**Scientific conduct and language must always abide by the laws of science.*

**Just as pagans can distort the laws of God with improper language and interpretation, so too can the perversionist distort the laws of God with these same tools.*

As it is with the word of God, there can only be one language of science, for without such a standard, each scientist could set his own conditions irrespective of the truth. Without this universal language, no scientific claim can ever be validated. Not surprisingly it can be demonstrated that scientific claims that attack God are always contrary to the universal language of science.

The Perversion of Science

Let's take a closer look at how the corruption of both scientific language and laws is being used against people of faith.

It is no secret that people of faith accept the Ten Commandments to be the laws of God. Isn't it amazing though that even non-believers who scoff at Christianity unwittingly believe and generally obey commandments such as *Thou shalt not steal, Thou shalt not kill, and Honor thy father and thy mother?*

Why is this?

The non-believer will argue that it is simply his good nature that causes him to obey God's word, but this is not true because long before any police department, social program or community organizing was ever organized, these words were laid down to us by God. They were taught to us, and we were indoctrinated with them. Indeed, who today other than the mentally impaired do not know that it is wrong to murder? The animal does not know this, but all men, because this language was brought to us by God, know that we must obey it.

In the same way that individuals must obey the language of God, so too, all discovery, theory and observation must obey the language of science.

When our language, our words, conflict with that of God and/or of science then we are driven by self-importance and agenda, and not by righteousness.

Just as it is with the word of God, our illiteracy in the language of science often leaves us vulnerable to being misled by lies and misrepresentations. The perversionist always exploits such vulnerability and never chooses to provide clarity and education.

Some of the most famous theories of civilization serve as eye-opening examples of just how the distortion of language can lead us to accept conjecture as etched-in-stone science.

It may surprise you to know that the concepts of gravity, electricity and magnetism have never been explained, nor for that matter ever proven by any scientist. Still, because we do not understand the language of science, we believe these theories to be true.

Naysayers may ask how I can say that the *general theory of gravity* is not proven. They may challenge me by stating, "I will surely fall to my death if I jump off a building." Doesn't this prove the theory? Well, no, it doesn't, and herein lies an important hurdle to understanding the language of science.

In the example of jumping off a building, the reason objects fall is because of a demonstrable physical law of nature. We can experience without exception that in the absence of resistance all objects fall and accelerate at the identical and constant rate of roughly 9.8 meters-second-second. However, up to this very day man remains unable to equate the laws of a falling object to the theories of gravity.

The various theories of gravity only attempt to explain why this law applies but we still don't know why. Newton and Einstein had no more clues to answering this than you and I.

Lest you think me out of my mind, a simple Internet search will show that in both quantum physics and astronomical physics, all theories of gravity fail to hold true, and the "experts" are still looking for that truth.[15]

Accordingly, to fortify our fluency in the universal language of science we must commit the following statement to memory.

---

15   https://www.nbcnews.com/mach/science/einstein-showed-newton-was-wrong-about-gravity-now-scientists-are-ncna1038671.

The Perversion of Science

"No existing scientific theory has ever been proven."

A short detour here into a real-world phenomenon should illuminate how important it is to keep both language and law accurate and in concert with each other.

In our world it is common for individuals to defend abortion, sexual perversion, and other sins by twisting God's language and misinterpreting laws. Frequently the pagan will quote Scripture to suggest that God supports his immorality. A good example follows.

<u>Psalm 145:9</u>

The Lord is good to all and his mercy is over all that he has made.

Not only does the pagan quote this type of Scripture to justify his perversion as being accepted by our all-loving God, but he also casts us as hypocrites for not accepting it.

However, when we cite additional, clarifying Scripture that explains the full intentions of God, such as the citation below, the pagan will close his ears and double down on his accusations of our hypocrisy.

<u>Mark 16:16</u>

Whoever believes and is baptized will be saved, but whoever does not believe will be condemned.

In the world of science, it is this exact behavior of distorting language and law that the perversionist uses to attack our faith. The pagan and the scientific perversionist are of the same fraternity.

Now, let us get back to the specific topic of scientific language and behavior as it applies to theories.

Depending on one's point of view, a scientific theory can be labeled as a guess, a hunch, or even a belief. Good theories are based on sound data, observation, and documentation, but at the end of the day we must steadfastly understand that *no currently active scientific theory has ever been proven*; we must not be fooled.

Many believe that once a theory is proven it becomes a law. This is not true. The debate of scientific law versus scientific theory has caused more than one participant to become confused, angered, and argumentative.

Be advised, almost without exception, the proponents of various scientific theories, especially ones that attack God, are militant in insisting that their conclusions are indefatigable truth.

It is important for us to never allow our faith or beliefs to be challenged by a theory, no matter how impressive the presentation.

There are many opinions and writings that explain the difference between a scientific law and a scientific theory. I am not going to cite any of these definitions but instead will give you my own. I believe they will help you separate fact from fiction as you pursue your own scientific journey.

<u>Scientific theory</u>: A collection of observations, calculations and ideas brought together that attempt to explain physical phenomena (e.g., the general theory of gravity).

<u>Theoretical science</u>: A collection of observations, calculations and ideas brought together to explain physical claims that have never been witnessed or documented (e.g., the big bang theory).

<u>Scientific law</u>: Physical behaviors repeatedly observed in nature that may or may not have defined scientific explanations; scientific laws have no exceptions or contradictions. For example, at standardized atmospheric conditions water will always freeze at 32 °F.

The Perversion of Science

The best scientific theories are ones designed as solutions to a problem. For example, someone once theorized that an inflatable car airbag would save lives. The airbag was built and tested with proven results. As a result, the theory was no longer needed. Because airbags were successfully tested and used, we now have scientific airbag laws and language (instructions) that can be followed by others to replicate the construction of new airbags.

In this example both the laws and language of airbag science are presented in harmony. They complement each other. Unfortunately, science is not always presented in this manner. Frequently, it is the language of science that is perverted to confuse us and create doubts about God's promises.

The language of science

Perhaps the easiest to demonstrate an example of perverted scientific language comes into play within the pursuit of life on other planets. Let us follow an example of this language twisting.

It is a tenet of science that water is a necessary ingredient to support life. NASA routinely claims that if a planet has water, it is reasonable to believe that life at some point could have existed on that planet.[16] It is also accepted that without water a planet could not support life. At this point there is no disagreement.

Continuing, scientists have indeed found evidence of water on Mars.[17]

Accordingly, many, including NASA have concluded that the exploration of Mars is justified because the discovery of water indicates a strong possibility of life.

---

16   https://www.nasa.gov/vision/universe/solarsystem/Water:_Molecule_of_Life.html.
17   https://www.livescience.com/water-found-beneath-mars.

It is at this point the language of science becomes perverted and the scientist begins to weave tall tales to support his agenda.

By itself, water will not give rise to life. Many other complex conditions must exist with water for life to emerge and thrive. On earth water is an active part of our ecosystem with many moving parts.[18] It is full of nutrients, oxygen yielding/CO_2-consuming plants and organisms. It is home to many species of animals, it is temperature and pH controlled, and most importantly, it constantly evaporates, then cools and nourishes the planet with rains. Water and the winds cause currents that cleanse the planet and naturally plants seeds and pollen as far as the eye can see, bringing with it life-sustaining plant life.

Conversely, the water on Mars is of no such complexity. The water on Mars is largely trapped in ice. When the planet warms the ice melts for a short time and makes a big puddle. When the temperature drops the water freezes back into ice.[19] The water on Mars is as dead as the rest of the iron-impregnated rocks responsible for us naming it "the Red Planet."

Please understand, I acknowledge completely that theories are the very seeds of scientific discovery. Good theories pave the path to better lives for mankind. For our welfare and benefit, sound theoretical research must be supported, funded, and nourished by our government, our schools and by the public.

However, when it comes to things like renewable energy, climate change, life on other planets, or the origin of life, anti-Christian theorists purposely skirt the language of science and promote these claims without ever having to face truthful scrutiny.

---

18   https://sciencing.com/role-water-ecosystem-5444202.htm.
19   https://www.nasa.gov/feature/episode-18-we-asked-a-nasa-scientist-is-there-water-on-mars.

With your help, those days will soon be no more. To become even more fluent in the universal language, I would like you to also commit this axiom to memory.

"No scientific discovery has ever contradicted the laws of science."

Let's take a quick diversion and examine how a scientific theory can be made to look credible on the surface, but then, upon a closer, scientifically savvy examination, be illuminated as nothing more than fiction. This is exactly how the perversionist attacks people of faith.

Imagine that I wanted to put forward a theory explaining the life and physical laws surrounding a hypothetical super athlete who will one day in the future be able to run forty-five miles per hour.

Scientifically, I could calculate how many calories he would need to perform. I could predict the wear and tear on his joints, his required muscle-to-fat ratio, his heart performance, the demands on his lungs, the friction of passing air on his skin, the type of shoe he would need, how far he could run before exhaustion, and I could even make sensible speculations on what type of career opportunities would be open to him.

Based on hard science I could indeed put forward a credible document on the morphology of this theoretical man.

However, even though my calculations and projections would all be scientifically accurate, the reality is that no man is ever going to run forty-five miles per hour because the laws of biology, genetics, anatomy, physics, and physiology show this level of athleticism to be beyond the capabilities of bone, muscle, organs, and ligaments. Smart scientists would quickly expose my theory as fiction.

We can adopt the following axiom as an indefatigable rule

or measure when assessing any scientific claim, especially the apocalyptic ones.

No scientific discovery, claim, theory, or observation can ever be given credibility unless all the data collected, both supportive and contradictory, are always transparent and readily available.

How can we not be doubtful of theories such as climate change when any dissenting voices or research is squashed and labeled as conspiratorial?

The perversionist will never admit that there are some things in life that are beyond his ability to understand. To do so would, in many cases, prevent him from obtaining funding for future research. Even worse, it would force him to admit that there is a God.

I believe that one of the most noble things we Christians can do is to hold these evil people accountable to both the laws of God and of science.

Chapter Three

Clean, Renewable, Sustainable Energy

One of the sharpest swords Satan has thrust into our midst is the concept that we need to find clean, renewable, and sustainable sources of energy. On the surface these goals seem wholesome and in keeping with God's instructions that we are good caretakers of the planet. How could this possibly be a perversion of science; how could this possibly be an attack on God?

I promise you, the belief that earth is running out of energy, and that man faces extinction unless he can find cleaner, renewable, sustainable energy is a horrible, purposeful deception. The belief that we are on a path to one day run out of energy is a scientific impossibility.

This scare over energy is crippling the American economy and hurting the American family. It is eliminating jobs, raising our cost of goods, placing doubt in the financial markets, and causing men to spend undue resources and effort trying to fulfill needs that are already being met very well by current technology. As we will also discover, this energy scare is an attack on God.

Unfortunately, the topic of energy is not only complex and multifaceted but is also rarely presented to the public in an open forum without bias due to the unfathomable money and power surrounding the subject. Energy decisions touch many aspects of our lives, and we must demand higher standards for how information on the topic is presented.

As a starting point for this chapter, let us recognize and acknowledge that the terminology *source of energy* whether we call it clean, sustainable, or renewable is scientifically incorrect. We learned from *the law of conservation of energy* that energy cannot be made or destroyed. We also learned that the only thing man can do with energy is to convert it from one form to another. Therefore, the categorization of any process or fuel as a source of energy is faulty. Going forward, we must begin speaking about energy within the proper terminology of *energy conversion processes*.

Let us first examine from a scriptural standpoint exactly how this frantic worry over future energy needs is blasphemy.

This worry not only maintains that God didn't bestow enough energy on mankind, but it also maintains that what energy he did give us is dirty, polluting, and harmful to man.

To think God created all things but wasn't smart enough to give us proper energy resources is ridiculous. Would a loving mother ever pack spoiled food into her child's lunch box? Of course, she wouldn't! Yet as preposterous as that idea is, the authors of these theories want us to believe that God created a poisoned earth.

Even more insulting and blasphemous is the perversionist's pompous suggestion that man has the wisdom, knowledge, and power to improve, fix and save God's Creation. Christians know that in *Matthew 6:26* God promised us that he would provide everything we need. We must understand that energy was included in that promise. Impressively, we again see God's promise to provide for us in the Scripture below.

Matthew 6:31–33 ESV

Therefore, do not be anxious, saying, "What shall we eat?" or "What shall we drink?" or "What shall we wear?" For the Gentiles seek after all these things, and your heavenly Father knows that you need them all. But seek first the kingdom of God and his righteousness, and all these things will be added to you.

One important part of the energy equation that most likely will forever separate Christians from non-believers is the matter of worry. A Christian believes that God will provide while the pagan, terrified over the vision of running out of oil frantically asks us, "With oil in finite supply, how can you not worry about our future?"

The answer to this is simple. God never promised us an endless supply of any single thing. His promise is that we will have everything we need. Our faith tells us that in his abundance God has already made way for the next set of geniuses and technologies that will guide us into the future. In addition, sustaining us does not require that life in the future includes low-cost airfare, automobiles, Internet, or any other conveniences that we have today.

The worry and fanaticism over vanishing energy is not based in science; it is based in Satan casting worry in the hearts and minds of men.

The specific purpose of this chapter is to reassure the reader that the only thing God wants us to do with energy sources is to use them to live fruitful, fulfilling lives, and to help others. The salient point I want us to understand is that it is foolish and scientifically wrong to believe that any form of energy conversion is better at sustaining us.

Energy sources should be viewed identically as items in the grocery store. We choose what works, we clean up after ourselves, and then when we need more, the grocer will have restocked the shelves. Brands may come and go, but always the shelves are full. God is our energy "grocer."

Scripture and energy science go together, and a little deeper look exposes just how fraudulent the worry over energy is.

It is fundamental to remember and hold fast that the only source of energy available to man and to planet earth is the sun. It is pure, clean, and so constant that it continues to sustain our existence. The energy from the sun is stored in countless forms, and all of it is available to us through one process or another. The following analogy will establish a foundation with which we can better understand energy.

Your job is your source of income; your checking account is the place where your money is stored. Your checking account surely is not your source of money, because if you lose your job, your checking account could not provide any continuing benefit to you.

In the same way, the sun is our source of energy. Things like oil, gas, and wind are merely what have been deposited in our "energy checking account." Like our jobs, if the sun keeps making deposits in our "energy checking account" we can continue making "withdrawals" of energy from the various places it is stored for us. If the sun is alive, then the amount of energy available to us will remain constant, fixed, steady and dependable for the duration of our existence.

In addition to this clarification, we must understand that no energy conversion is clean, not even something as beautiful as our own functioning human bodies. All conversions of energy create waste, and if we begin to analyze and compare energy conversions from a true, scientific perspective with all personal agendas put aside, what we will uncover is that much of what we thought was clean and good for the environment is often not quite as wonderful as we hoped for. In many instances the new and improved product is as much or even more harmful than the so-called dirty energy conversion process that it replaced.

When we examine scientific comparisons of energy conversion technology it is imperative that we make conclusions only after undergoing a true apples-to-apples comparison that considers all the variables. There will always be a temptation by the person making a presentation to show only the results that support the points he wants to make. While this is human nature, we must not be duped. As we continue to analyze the real science of energy, let's pull from our toolbox the tools of *comparative numbers, equilibrium, standardized data,* and *the conservation of energy* to deflate the scare over energy.

The following hypothetical example illustrates just how easily the perversionist of science can manipulate data to mislead us and influence us to accept a new energy technology that is not really all that it is cracked up to be.

Imagine a test that is being done to determine the pollution factor of two different fuels. Let's call them fuels A and B. It is reported to us that after testing a gallon each of fuels A and B, fuel A produced twice as much pollution as fuel B. The results are then published, and the new product is advertised and sold accordingly. We are enticed by the claim that fuel B is 50 percent less polluting than fuel A. To a reasonable man this sounds like a fair comparison, and we would all get in line to purchase fuel B.

In this hypothetical case, however, a closer look at the data reveals that this fuel comparison is misleading. Upon closer examination of the data, we discover it takes five gallons of fuel B to release the same amount of energy as fuel A. This information changes the entire ramification of this study because a gallon-to-gallon comparison would not be fair. Let's look at how different the results would be when we make an apples-to-apples comparison that requires both fuels to deliver the same amount of energy. In all scientific studies, we begin with the up-front information that we know to be factual. This is universally called "given information" or more commonly, "given."

Given:

One gallon of fuel A = 2 pollution units
One gallon of fuel B = 1 pollution unit

New discovery:

One gallon of fuel A = 30 energy units (30 EUs)
Five gallons of fuel B = 30 energy units (30 EUs)

Therefore, we can produce thirty EUs in two different ways:

(1 gallon of fuel that emits 2 pollution units per gallon)

OR

(5 gallons of fuel B that emits 1 pollution unit per gallon)

Results:

Fuel A generates 2 pollution units to produce 30 EUs
Fuel B generates 5 pollution units to produce 30 EUs

So, you see, while the initial gallon-to-gallon presentation leads us to believe that fuel B is cleaner, a proper scientific comparison demonstrates that fuel A, the traditional fuel, is much cleaner.

For impact purposes, remember that if this scenario happened in real life, all the workers involved with manufacturing, transporting, testing, promoting, and distributing fuel A would lose their jobs and their livelihoods would be put in jeopardy. We would then be left to consume fuel B, which causes more overall pollution.

Because changes in our energy choices can ruin lives and turn thriving communities into ghost towns, it is vitally important that we reject energy changes that are driven by political agenda and profit goals. When energy choices are based on the natural resources God gave to us, the needs of mankind, and honest science, we soon come to learn that most "save the planet technologies" are not in our best interests.

In real-life energy comparisons, the variables can be very complicated, and while I surely don't mean to insult anyone with my over-simplified exercise, the fact remains that all too often a complete disclosure of energy truth is not presented to us. Again, this is because the new energy technology is driven by agenda and cannot stand on its own merits. Many of these so-called sustainable technologies will only be accepted by the public under the pressures of fear and perverted statistics.

The stakes are now too high for us not to dig deeper, to demand more thorough explanations, and to better understand all the ramifications of what is being presented to us.

An excellent real-life tool we can use to truly expose all the pros and cons of a new energy technology is a process known as mass balance (also energy balance).[20] Mass/energy balance examines scientific claims in a manner that leaves no stone unturned. The perversionist loathes and avoids these processes like the plague.

Mass/energy balance exposes bad science and demands that we answer all the right questions. What was done to the earth to create the new technology? Did producing the new technology require

---

20   https://pages.mtu.edu/~reh/courses/ce251/251_notes_dir/node3.html.

pollution-generating machines and processes? Did manufacturing the new technology require the use of already precious and limited resources? Are the costs of the new technology represented to be artificially lower than existing technologies because of an unfair advantage provided by governmental financial aid? How much new pollution is generated in the transportation and transmission of this new technology?

The list of these important questions goes on and on, but one thing is for certain, if we do not require new scientific claims to hold up to the standards of mass/energy balance, our world will continue to grow more vulnerable to the whims and desires of those with personal agendas and hate for God's promises.

I hope that my simple exercise serves as a guideline and a reminder to all of us to press for more details, to ask questions and to demand direct answers.

Let us now move from the general to the specific using some actual examples of how data is being perverted to promote energy technologies that are not as beneficial to us as represented. All these so-called clean and renewable energy sources have hidden, harmful components.

<u>Solar energy</u>

Anyone who has seen a solar farm will tell you that they are pleasing to the eye. Their orderly, shiny, and pristine appearance quickly instills a popular, easily sellable, albeit artificial perception that building more solar farms is an effective way to help the environment and reduce our dependence on fossil fuels, especially the foreign variety.

Left up to the current purveyors, including our government, media, and environmental activists, this is the only view of solar technology that the public would ever see. However, if we examine the entire story about solar technology, a different view emerges.

If a perversionist speaks to you about solar technology, consider it your scientific and biblical responsibility to stop them in their tracks with proper rebuttals.

The first thing that supporters of solar energy conversion don't want us to know is that the manufacture of solar panels is a filthy, toxic, hazardous, waste-generating process. It generates chemical waste that winds up back in our environment in one form or another.

The metals, hydrocarbon-rich plastics and caustic chemicals required to manufacture panels generate tens of millions of gallons of EPA-classified F006 hazardous waste, much of it carcinogenic. Currently large volumes of this waste are being transported under great risk to waste handling facilities both in the US and abroad.

When we weigh the minuscule fraction of energy usage provided by solar conversion against the amount of pollution generated by the process, we begin to scratch the surface of this environmentally unfriendly technology.

Consider that the F006 waste must be transported using fossil fuel-burning vehicles, treated in plants that consume fossil fuels, and once neutralized, transported to disposal sites once again using vehicles that burn fossil fuels. Suddenly, the carbon footprint of solar panels seems a little bigger than we have been led to believe.

Furthermore, the manufacture of solar panels is a resource-devouring process. The minerals and chemicals required must be mined and stripped from the earth thereby exposing water supplies, land, and air to toxic, even carcinogenic contamination.

The popular objections to America's use of fossil fuels are largely centered on a perverted worry over depleting a limited resource, causing a larger carbon footprint, damaging the earth, particularly topical geography, and water supplies, and putting other toxins into the environment.

Proponents of solar technology, along with the public, must be shown that this technology also violates every one of these environmental concerns.

I want to make it perfectly clear that I am not trying to push any energy conversion technology over another. My belief is that negative environmental effects should all be addressed regardless of the technology with which they were created. To honor science, Scripture, and our environment, we must be just as critical of the downsides of all new energy technologies as we are the ones we seek to minimize or eliminate. In the case of solar technology, the scientific evidence tells us that it contaminates a significant amount of water and creates carcinogenic waste. Facts like these can no longer be hidden from the public at the expense of protecting perversionist agendas.

Since I mentioned the resource-hungry nature of solar panel manufacturing, I thought it would be a good idea to review the environmentally aggressive process involved. The resources solar technology requires are mind-boggling.

The following list cites the natural resources that are consumed in the manufacture of solar panels. I invite you to first examine the list and then judge for yourself if solar energy conversion is the wonderful, God-correcting process that some would have you believe.

- Iron ore for steel production

- Aluminum for casings and mechanical parts
- Cadmium used in the solar cell
- Boron for the construction of computer chips
- Coal, oil, natural gas used to power the factories processing these materials
- Copper for wiring and electrical contacts and lines of transmission to grid network
- Gallium and arsenic used in the semiconductor/processors that control the panels
- Indium used in solar cells
- Molybdenum used to energize the cells
- Lead, lithium, cadmium all used in batteries
- Silica for glass
- Selenium
- Titanium
- Pure water

Additional metals used, depending on the specific process, can include nickel, chromium, tellurium, and others. In addition, the decorative processes used to add an attractive appearance, especially in consumer market products, also creates toxic, hazardous electroplating, and painting waste.

The point of this list is to make the perversionist who promotes solar technology live by the standard of "what's good for the goose is good for the gander." If the supposed shortcomings of traditional energy conversion processes include stripping of the land, recklessly consuming precious resources, and creating pollution, then solar technology must also be exposed as an egregious offender of these very same environmental sins.

I believe that discussions about solar energy conversion carry important implications and responsibilities to both people of faith and to non-believers.

To my fellow Christians, if you believe as I do that in *Genesis 1:26*, God asks us to be good caretakers of his Creation, then you have no choice but to accept the responsibility for acquiring a better understanding of energy conversion technologies and spread the word about how the resources God gave us are already clean, renewable, and sustainable.

To non-believers and pagans, if your zeal to protect the environment is pure and true, then you can no longer purposefully look the other way at environmental havoc simply because the technology you favor suits your political or personal agenda.

The next important characteristic of solar energy conversion we should review is actual energy output. The proponents of solar energy conversion and other so-called clean conversion processes must be made to come clean with the public and provide honest, unbiased kilowatt-to-kilowatt, apples-to-apples, toxicity-to-toxicity, and cost-to-cost comparisons. It is only through creating an open and honest playing field that average Americans can have an authoritative voice in determining our future energy policies.

Continuing our examination of solar energy conversion, I can say without fear of repercussion that regardless of where you get your statistics, you will find it widely accepted within the scientific community that solar energy cannot and will not ever have a significant impact on cleaning (saving?) our environment or supplying a significant part of our energy conversion needs.

Let us not marginalize solar technology but instead put it in its proper perspective. If we are going to allow a technology to destroy jobs, shut down communities, and literally turn society upside down we owe it to each other to understand all the facts.

The contribution solar technology offers civilization is important but also very limited. It is certainly not going to "save" the planet or anything else for that matter. Don't take my word for it. Let's use our science toolbox to compare a solar farm to a nuclear power plant to reveal just how impotent this new "wonder" technology really is. I believe that this real-world exercise will be an eye-opener.

To begin this comparison, we will first need to lock in on three vitally important and universally accepted conventions used to analyze power-generating facilities.

- The most common unit of measurement for a power plant is the watt. However, because the wattage produced is so large, output is always expressed with mathematical multiplication prefixes. A kilowatt is one thousand watts, a megawatt is one million watts, and a gigawatt is one billion watts.

- The wattage rating of any power plant is only reflective of the maximum, instantaneous power that can be produced by that plant operating at ideal conditions and full operation. It doesn't tell us anything about the cumulative power that is produced at any given time during the day.

- The time component of power production is additional information that is mandatory to make a proper comparison between two or more power-generating facilities. The common designation for this information is kilowatt-hour/megawatt-hour. Take care in understanding that the designation kilowatt-hour is not the same as kilowatt-per-hour (kilowatt/hr).

  - The kilowatt per hour designation (kw/hr) is meant to indicate how much energy can be produced in one hour. Remember, not all power-generating facilities operate twenty-four hours per day.

- The kilowatt-per-hour designation is employed to indicate that the generating facility produces x-number of kilowatts on a continuous, ongoing basis, twenty-four hours per day.

With this information at hand, let us now compare the total power produced in a solar farm versus a nuclear plant.

1. According to the United States Nuclear Regulatory Commission,[21] the Palo Verde Nuclear Generating Station can produce up to 3,990 megawatts of electricity. This translates into 3,990,000,000 watts, or roughly 4 gigawatts.

2. According to the Clean Energy Collective,[22] the solar panel farm at the Aurora, Colorado/Arapahoe County solar farm uses 1,684 panels installed on a 4.5-acre site to produce 498 kilowatts of instantaneous power. This translates into 498,000-hour watts.

For ease of comparison let's round off these numbers.

- The Palo Verde nuclear plant produces a maximum of 4,000,000,000 instantaneous watts of power (4 billion watts).

- The Aurora Colorado/Arapahoe County solar farm produces a maximum 500,000 maximum instantaneous watts of power (one-half million watts).

The first eye-opening revelation is that the nuclear plant can produce eight thousand times more instantaneous power than the solar farm at its theoretical maximum output. Comparative

---

21   http://www.nrc.gov/info-finder/reactor/palo1.html.
22   https://www.solardaily.com/reports/Community_Solar_Coming_to_City_of_Aurora_and_Arapahoe_County_999.html.

numbers then tell us that it will require eight thousand solar farms the size of the nuclear plant to match the instantaneous power contribution of just one nuclear plant for the sizes of the plants we are comparing.

But wait, there is more. To make our comparison accurate, we need to call up the kilowatt-hour designation I mentioned earlier. It has great significance in this comparison.

The nuclear plant produces its power twenty-four hours per day, seven days per week. So, this plant is not only a 4-gigawatt facility, but also a 4-gigawatt-hour facility.

Conversely, the solar plant only produces its maximum power when the sun is maximally available. When we take into consideration cloud interference, shorter periods of sunlight in the winter and the sunrise-sunset periods where sunlight is not particularly strong, it is safe to say that a solar facility only produces maximum energy at an inflated best for eight hours per day. This dynamic causes the solar facility to suffer greatly when compared to traditional forms of energy production.

While the Arapahoe facility is indeed a 500-kilowatt maximum capacity generating facility, we must note that because it only produces power for one-third as many hours as a twenty-four-hour plant, maximum output averages it out to be only a 166-kilowatt-hour facility, and that is only when the sun is at its most unobstructive and raging presence.

The complete analysis now reveals that to equal the power-generating capacity of the nuclear plant in question, we would have to build twenty-four thousand solar farms the size of the Aurora/Arapaho facility (4 billion watts/plant divided by 166,666 watts = 24,000 solar plants).

Let us look at the tale of the tape so far.

Nuclear = 4,000,000,000 watts-hour producing energy twenty-four hours per day

Solar = 166,666 watts-hour producing energy eight hours per day

Clearly, the building of solar farms does not seem like a "God-correcting," viable solution to our massive energy needs.

Please note that the case for solar is even weaker than just described.

The theoretical output that I awarded to the Aurora Colorado/Arapaho County solar facility was in all honesty overly generous to what the facility produces. The truth is that it could possibly require sixty thousand or more Aurora-sized solar plants to equal the electricity produced by one nuclear plant. The reason for this is that even during the day when the sun is out, the solar facility does not routinely reach its stated maximum capacity. Clouds and storms impact the output of solar farms significantly.

At the time this chapter was written there was a website where one could see actual current energy production of the facility.

On several visits to that site, I found the facility generating as little 127,000 watts of instantaneous energy. I can only guess that the reason the site is no longer active is that inquiring minds like mine looked at the dismal daily production and exposed the same flaws I discovered. Again, you see, the perversionist avoids the truth at all expenses.

For argument's sake, however, let us do an actual calculation based on the active performance of this plant at the time I checked in on it.

<u>Given:</u>

The Perversion of Science

- Palo Verde, current daily output: 3,900,000,000 w-h

- Aurora/Arapaho current output: 127,000 watts
  Converted to w-hr by dividing by 3 = 42,333 w-hr (this considers the plant only operates eight hour/day

As crazy as it sounds, based on the actual production on that day, it would take 3.9 billion ÷ 42,333 = 92,126 of these solar plants to equal the daily output of our nuclear plant.

We should be curious about what 92,126 of these solar farms would look like.

Consider that the nuclear plant occupies about ten acres of real estate. While the individual solar plant occupies only 4.5 acres per plant. Therefore, to achieve the same power output as the nuclear plant with solar energy we would need (92,126 solar plants) x (4.5 acres per plant) = 414,567 acres.

In common terms, this means a solar plant would have to be twice the size of New York City or 1.3 times the size of Los Angeles to equal the power output of our nuclear power plant. The ramifications of this comparison are mind-boggling and expose just how corrupt perversionist theory is.

While this was a long exercise, it demonstrates how real science works. The toolbox tools enable us to slice, dice and pare any scientific claim down to where it is standardized, comparative, and can be analyzed in an unbiased fashion.

It also demonstrates how technology is being misrepresented to attack God, to claim that the resources he gave us are diminishing, and how we must develop new technologies to save his planet.

As a side note, in the proper setting, solar technology can provide us with valuable, albeit limited utility. The panels, once installed, will always be there to provide service to mankind. In simple applications such as landscape lighting where the cost of initial investment is minor, it doesn't require payback. In addition, solar technology can be a savior in areas that do not have traditional energy conversion technology available.

However, playing solar technology as a trump card over God's perfect Creation, a Creation that includes fossil fuels, nuclear technology and other bountiful fuel sources cannot go uncontested.

<u>Wind power – more warming than fossil fuel</u>

To understand how wind technology is being used to attack God and our faith we must take a closer look at both the wind, and windmill power conversion.

Like solar farms, wind turbine farms present a clean, orderly appearance that leaves the casual observer with the impression that he witnessed something good for the environment. There is some truth to such observations, and I will openly admit that applied properly, wind turbine technology can indeed make some contribution, but not substantial, to our need for energy conversion technologies. In remote areas of the world, wind farms can be a welcome gift.

However, wind technology is not going to impact mankind to any crucial degree. It is a niche technology, an amusement, an option that makes sense here and there.

To be fair, we should consider the positive operational advantages of this conversion technology. The actual wind conversion process itself—wind-turning propellers that turn generators—is clean and non-polluting. It is also a more dependable technology than solar because wind is much more readily available than full, unobstructed sunshine. We know that while over short periods of time wind patterns may fluctuate, over long periods of time wind currents are consistent and dependable. We can comfortably predict that a turbine will deliver close to its officially rated output capacity over the time of its predicted lifespan.

Of the publicized and documented downsides of this technology there are accounts of the damage turbines can do to birds. Additionally, during the time of day when the sun is low in the sky, the rotating blades can create stroboscopic effects that have rendered drivers unable to see the road. We are also aware that the manufacture of windmills, like all other manufacturing processes, utilizes precious raw materials and requires fossil fuel-hungry equipment to mine, build and transport the units.

The more alarming downside of windmill farms, however, is the depletion of natural, life-sustaining winds from our environment. This is an ill effect that others have ignored, and regardless of your personal position on global warming, without argument, wind turbine technology does produce the negative, warming effects on our climate that climate change proponents are supposedly averse to.

Our toolbox concepts of *equilibrium* and *conservation* will shed some much-needed light on how capturing wind for energy conversion presents its own set of very real and dangerous pollution and environmental downsides.

Let's first consider how God incorporated the natural, protective forces of wind into his Creation. This part of his work is truly breathtaking, and it demands scientific understanding.

The great winds of earth protect us by providing many cooling benefits to our planet, benefits far more wonderous than a simple, refreshing summer breeze on a hot, sunny golf course.

Whenever we travel, and especially by plane, if we take a simple glance out the window, as far as our eyes can see, even in the most remote, desolate, uninhabited lands, we behold countless miles and acres of trees, bushes, flowers, weeds, and lush greenery beyond the imagination.

While we stare in amazement, we generally don't stop to ask ourselves, "Who planted all this stuff?"

The answer is very simple. The wind did this. Some like to call it Johnny Appleseed, but it is largely the wind that did all this. It did it by carrying pollen, seeds, water, and nutrients to all corners of the earth, constantly reforesting our beautiful, bountiful planet. Of course, the bees, birds, and insects also contribute to this, but for now let us keep our conversation focused on the wind. (Isn't it just like God to steal the show, throwing even more bounty at us than we know what to do with?)

What we must now absorb and be aware of is that every waking moment of every day all this greenery undertakes the work of photosynthesis. This is the process whereby plants use carbon dioxide, sunlight, and water to manufacture sugars, purify our air and provide life-giving oxygen. This miracle of nature has a constant cooling effect on the planet, to say nothing of enabling man to breathe, eat, make medicines and otherwise flourish.

The next time that spring pollen blows in our eyes, irritates our nose, or covers our car in a dusty blanket, it is good for us to remember that this is God's hand reforesting our planet. I promise you, God has provided so many natural sustainability tools into Creation, as you read further you will surely scoff at any man, scientist or layman, who suggests that our planet is not sustainable, or that man has any ability whatsoever to guide its path.

The Perversion of Science

Now let us look at one of the most severe detriments of wind technology. A detriment that the world-saving, God-hating apocalypse-spreading perversionist doesn't want us to consider.

It is incorrect to assume that wind is any more free, clean, and renewable than any of the other sources of energy conversion God has provided. To believe this is to pervert science.

There is a finite amount of wind on earth. As the laws of conservation tell us, we cannot generate something out of nothing. In the case of turbines, they absorb the energy from the wind leaving much less wind at the exit of the blades. This is not any different than a hydroelectric plant, which takes the energy from a raging river, converts it to electricity and then releases a very tame, low-energy stream of water. Same principle. Same science.

So, we see the first non-green, global-warming characteristic of wind technology. The more turbines we build, the more wind currents we take out of the environment. The more wind currents we remove from the environment, the less wind is available for reforestation.

I hope by now you are starting to see how the laws of science, which are the laws of God, quickly dismantle these idiotic theories that man can and must save the planet. There will be no scientific perversion allowed to stand within the covers of this book, and hopefully also not between the ears of the reader.

Now, for those pagans and deniers who do not believe that wind farms warm the planet by diminishing our wind currents, and others who just would like to see this in action, I have designed a little experiment for you.

Gather these materials: a small electric fan, four to six toy pinwheels that you can usually find in a dollar/bargain store, six wine or soda bottles, some sand, and six corks. We will conduct the experiment indoors where there is no interference from real wind.

Using a drill bit that is slightly smaller than the stick the toy pinwheel is mounted on, bore a hole by hand through each cork, as close to the center as possible. Next, fill all the bottles with sand so that they do not tip over during the experiment. After they are filled with sand, place a cork in each bottle and gently slide the stick of a pinwheel through the cork as far down as possible without causing the pinwheel to hit the fat part of the bottle; the pinwheel needs to turn freely.

Now comes the meat of this experiment. First align one of your turbines directly in front of the fan but a couple of feet back from it. Now do a test to make sure the fan is not too powerful for your pinwheel turbine. Move this pinwheel back to the point where it turns at a nice clip. You want it steady, but not on the verge of blowing over. Obviously the closer the pinwheel is to the fan, the faster it will turn.

Once you have the first pinwheel set in place, with the fan still running place a second pinwheel about two feet directly behind the first pinwheel. Then put a third and fourth, or however many you have made in the very same manner.

You are going to discover that each additional pinwheel you add to the back of the line will turn slower than the one in front. This experiment demonstrates that indeed wind farms deplete air currents, and as described demonstrate the same global warming properties that the perversionist claims are destroying our planet.

When we think of wind, we picture it as free, abundant, and limitless. However, just like water, oil, chromium or gold, there is a finite amount of wind on earth. Just like gasoline is depleted as our car motors run, wind is also consumed when it runs the engines of the wind turbine. I promise you, if your home sat at the back of the wind farm we just created, it would be a lot hotter than it was before your breezes were usurped.

Scripture pointed out to us long ago the science of our winds and our abundant vegetation. The perversionist has yet to learn and accept God's science.

<u>Genesis 1:29 ESV</u>

And God said, "Behold, I have given you every plant yielding seed that is on the face of all the earth, and every tree with seed in its fruit. You shall have them for food."

<u>Psalm 72:16 ESV</u>

May there be abundance of grain in the land; on the tops of the mountains may it wave; may its fruit be like Lebanon; and may people blossom in the cities like the grass of the field!

<u>John 3:8</u>

The wind blows where it wishes, and you hear its sound, but you do not know where it comes from or where it goes. So, it is with everyone who is born of the Spirit.

Another important aspect of our winds has to do with the evaporation of water from the surface of lakes, oceans, and rivers. This evaporation has an immediate cooling effect and eventually allows for the formation of rain.[23] Rain is, of course, another natural, cooling, built-in temperature control that God's Creation provides to us, and it does so without us ever having to lift a finger.

Using what we learned about wind and energy from our simple

---

23   https://scijinks.gov/rain/.

pinwheel experiment, let us look at another way in which this miracle earth-saving technology causes the same kind of warming that the fuels it is designed to replace produce.

To produce electricity, wind farm propellers must first absorb energy from the wind. The angle or pitch of the blades cause the propeller to turn. The turning propeller is attached to the shaft of a turbine, and the turbine subsequently turns a generator, which produces an electrical current. As the generating system captures wind and uses it to turn the turbine, it presents a resistance that the wind must overcome.

All these stages of friction and resistance cause the release of heat and reduce the efficiency of how much wind is converted into electricity.

Since we know that energy must always be conserved, and from the concept of equilibrium, we know that the total energy on both sides of an equation must equal each other. Energy cannot be made nor destroyed. So as with all other energy technologies, the fuel for wind turbines is not free, and there is waste, in the form of heat lost in the process.

If we simplify this as an equation, it looks something like this:

Given:

W = The force or energy of the wind current (potential energy)
$W2$ = The force of the wind after turning the propeller
E = Electricity generated by the turning turbine
$\Delta 1$ = Energy as heat, loss due to friction of air on propellers
$\Delta 2$ = Energy as heat, lost to friction of turbine and motor

$\underline{W = E + \Delta 1 + \Delta 2 + W2}$

Initial wind force = energy produced + heat of turbine + heat due to friction across propeller + leftover wind

If supporters of the perverted, clean energy and climate change agenda understood even the most basic science they could not possibly believe that taking wind, which cools the earth, trapping it, and then generating heat from it, is any better than current fuels and technologies that we use.

A fun way to see firsthand how turbines affect currents is to visit beautiful Niagara Falls, Ontario. If you have never been there, you simply must visit. The sights are breathtaking and surely you will see the creative genius of our Lord.

During the day, the water runs vigorously and unabated, delivering high decibel, mesmerizing swoosh sounds while casting mist up as far as the eye can see. At night, however, a lot of the water flow is directed to the nearby hydroelectric plant and the rage becomes a gentle, calming, soft white noise experience that can lull you to sleep.[24] If you are awake during this time, you can physically see the diminished water flow going over the falls.

The issue again is that wind is not a free, limitless resource without a waste component.

I am also not saying that wind generators have no place in our world because they do. In areas where conventional energy technologies are not readily available, wind conversion, like solar conversion, can be a very helpful technology.

The important point here is that the euphoria surrounding wind technology is driving public policy, government funding and media coverage while simultaneously hiding downsides that might

---

24   https://www.niagarafallstourism.com/blog/do-they-shut-off-the-falls-at-night/.

be harmful to man.

The scientific community, to my knowledge, hasn't addressed the warming aspects of wind generators, and they surely haven't produced any models to predict how many wind generators we could erect before experiencing adverse environmental effects. These warming effects should be studied, quantified, and shared before we put up too many more turbine farms.

True science must continue to be applied to new fads like wind power. Every one of the relentless perversionists' campaigns for so-called new earth-saving technologies is rooted in man's pride and unwillingness to accept that there are some phenomena surrounding our existence that science will never grasp, and that man cannot control. So goes this attack on God.

Compact fluorescent light bulbs (CFLs)

The principal reason for promoting CFLs is that they require less electrical power to deliver the same amount of light as an incandescent bulb.[25] The thought process is that by using a more energy-efficient product, we can reduce our overall need to produce electricity. While there are studies showing that CFLs are not as efficient as some would have us believe, the bulbs do in fact use less electricity than a comparably bright incandescent bulb.

The shortcoming of these products, however, sticks out like a sore thumb once people realize that there is no energy crisis, and there will never be an energy crisis. We can reference Scripture already

---

25   https://science.howstuffworks.com/environmental/green-tech/sustainable/cfl-bulb.htm?segment=hsw.003&-slaid=9344829301&s1cid=15222398384&s1agid=132552738674&s1kid=dsa-19959388920&utm_source=adwords&gclid=Cj0KCQi-AieWOBhCYARIsANcOw0zCmX1WAzK_ttCc2y07AfNDI9YI5laG-cf3T0MKCqBMCAVV5g7Wyy1AaAoNjEALw_wcB.

quoted and see that the entire frenzy around reducing energy consumption is again rooted in a hate for Christianity and a refusal to accept God's gift of abundance. From a logical standpoint, do you really believe that our choice of light bulbs can have a direct effect on God's Creation? Still, the perversionist marches on with his hoaxes.

Furthermore, those who promote CFLs also hide their real agenda, which is to close all coal production and coal-fired power plants under the fallacy that burning coal is polluting the atmosphere and oceans with mercury.

We must not make light of mercury exposure because in certain forms is highly toxic to us. Exposure to it causes brain damage, loss of vision, pregnancy problems, and in general is attributed to many serious health problems.[26]

Let us be clear, researchers have indeed found mercury contamination in fish, air, water, and land. However, contrary to what the perversionist would have us believe, only small amounts of it come from the burning of coal. Science shows us that most of the mercury found in our environment comes from volcanoes and wildfires.[27] Adding further insult to the attack on coal, research also shows us that the most concentrated mercury contamination in the US is not in the east where coal mines and coal-fired power plants are the most concentrated, but rather across the central and western parts of the nation where there are the most forests, solar and wind farms.

The reason this is so important is that coal, a gift to us from God, <u>is responsible </u>for the livelihood and prosperity of tens of millions

26   https://www.epa.gov/mercury/health-effects-exposures-mercury.
27   https://www.forbes.com/sites/alexepstein/2015/11/24/the-truth-about-coal-and-mercury/?sh=2e4331d24da0.

of people, providing not only jobs and security but also essential electricity.

The reason I am spending a good amount talking about coal, CFLs and mercury is that this is one of the most vile, egregious, and well-cloaked attacks on God. It cannot be allowed to stand as a light-hearted, feel-good effort in which we laugh at our acceptance of the goofy-looking light bulb because we have been hoodwinked into believing we are helping the planet.

I will stress again that coal came from God, so remember what we are talking about. We are being asked to accept a light bulb as a cure for God's failure in giving us coal.

It is in the full disclosure of details that we see the real health and environmental perversion in this attack.

Like coal, CFLs also contain a measurable and dangerous amount of mercury. By using CFLs, we are bringing this toxin into our homes, and we are introducing it to our loved ones, visitors, and pets with many dangerous and uncontrollable variables.

We should be outraged that on the one hand our leaders champion reducing toxic mercury through the elimination of coal-burning industries, but on the other hand ignore the dangers of mercury-laced CFLs solely to force-feed the public their hidden political and personal climate agendas.

Either mercury is toxic to humans, or it isn't. If the argument is that we shouldn't be putting it into our environment, we surely shouldn't be bringing it inside our homes and businesses. The proponents of CFLs would have you believe that their risk of exposure to harmful levels of mercury is minimal, even minuscule. Nothing could be further from the truth.

The Perversion of Science

One of the fallacies being spread by proponents of CFLs is that in the event of a breakage, the expected amount that we might inhale is only several micrograms: hardly a danger.[28]

Let me explain how this deliberate misinformation could be lethal. Depending on the manufacturer, a CFL has between four and five milligrams of total mercury.[29]

Proponents, including our own EPA, love to minimize the mercury hazard of these bulbs by pointing out that the average thermometer has much more mercury in it. Here again, science is perverted against us and we are being lied to.

During our conversation about numbers in chapter one, we made a clarification between watts and watt-hours. I also stressed the vital need for us to understand the relationships of numbers in order that we might make better judgments about scientific claims. This CFL discussion is a crucial example of exactly why we must gain a better understanding of numbers.

In the event of a CFL breakage, the amount of mercury in a bulb is only that—an amount. When we speak in terms of possible inhalation exposure, we need to know not only how much toxin the bulb contains, but also the size of the area contaminated by the toxin. Knowing both of these data points allows us to determine the concentration level of toxin. It is the concentration level of a poison that determines how lethal an exposure is.

---

28   https://blogs.edf.org/climate411/2007/07/31/cfl_mercury-2/#:~:text=Compact%20fluorescent%20light%20bulbs%20(CFLs,-contain%20mercury%20%E2%80%93%20a%20dangerous%20toxin.&text=The%20amount%20of%20mercury%20in,%2C%20only%20 4%2D5%20milligrams.

29   https://www.epa.gov/cfl/what-are-connections-between-mercury-and-cfls#:~:text=Mercury%2C%20an%20essential%20part%20 of,mercury%20in%20over%20100%20CFLs.

In minimizing the dangers of mercury exposure in CFLs, the perversionist often manipulates the possible conditions of how mercury dispersion might occur in the case of an at-home CFL breakage. He unscrupulously presents our potential mercury exposure to seem benign.

For instance, he postulates that not all four milligrams of mercury will be released, and then claims that what is released will be spread out over an area large enough so that the maximum potential exposure concentration is minimal.

The problem, however, is that no scientist can predict what the specific conditions of broken CFL mercury release is because the variables of how a bulb can break are limitless. Consider the examples below.

- Imagine while driving home your shopping bag tips and the eight CFL bulbs you purchased break. In that case you could inhale thirty to forty milligrams of mercury in the very confined space of your car.
- Imagine that a bulb breaks in your hand; in that case you might inhale the entire amount of mercury in the bulb.
- Imagine that a bulb falls to the floor and breaks right in front of your child who is playing; again, the entire amount of mercury could be inhaled.
- Realize also that most homeowners place their exhausted bulbs into the regular trash. Now imagine how much mercury exposure our sanitation workers will be subjected to when tossing that garbage bag around.
- Imagine how much mercury is going into our landfills, and how rains will leach it back into our environment.

In the hustle and bustle of our daily lives, all these scenarios and more are not just possible but are guaranteed to happen in one form or another.

The scientist who minimizes our risk and assures us a low risk of mercury inhalation from broken CFLs is unethical, irresponsible, and in my judgment, criminal and immoral. It is impossible for anyone to know the exact circumstances with which a CFL may break. Any unbiased study of the mercury risk due to breakage and improper disposal illuminates that these bulbs are not safer than burning coal, and emphatically present dangerous levels far beyond anything created by this long-standing fossil fuel staple of our lives.[30]

A quick Internet search on the protocol of how to handle CFL breakage in our homes should quickly send up red flags and have us all concerned about the health hazards of CFLs. As you research these methods, you will learn about how your carpet will need special cleaning and may have to be avoided for a while. You will learn about the need to treat your vacuum cleaner. You will learn to close your heating and air conditioning vents while doing the cleaning. You will learn special procedures for possible contamination of bedding, food serving items, washing machines, clothing, and furniture.

Can you name me one single gift from God that is as potentially toxic as these man-made CFL saviors of the planet?

We should be alarmed if not terrified that a government-mandated product comes packaged with Hazmat-type accident instructions.

We should be equally concerned and informed about whether every private and public building we visit has adhered strictly to

---

30   https://ec.europa.eu/health/scientific_committees/opinions_layman/mercury-in-cfl/en/mercury-cfl/l-3/2-release-health-effects.htm.

broken CFL disposal and cleaning procedures.

The proper disposal of expired and broken bulbs requires that the bulbs be carefully packaged and returned only to an authorized recycling center. It is foolish to believe that the average person is going to inconvenience himself with a trip to the recycling center in the middle of a hectic day. These unrealistic dynamics and expectations represent a clear, undeniable imminent danger to the health and welfare of future generations.

Surely as I am writing this book, the majority of expired CFLs are being put into the common trash and sent to our landfills. And why not? After all, we have been disposing of light bulbs this way for years, and our government tells us every day that these bulbs are safe and harmless. If the bulbs are safe, why do we need special disposal?

I may not be the first to say this, but I will say it the loudest. At some point in the not-too-distant future, because the majority of our used CFLs are being sent to common landfills, the resulting leakage of mercury into our land and water supplies will take the health of many Americans. It could potentially be a larger problem than asbestos.

In a manner like the infamous progression of thalidomide, asbestos and lead paint, the risks of which were all minimized to us by our leaders, the mercury terror of CFLs, if not addressed, will rise, and wreak similar horrible health consequences across the globe.

At the risk of repeating myself, I cannot stress enough that promoting CFLs to save earth from God-given fossil fuels doesn't just attack Christianity, it also jeopardizes the careers, health, life and welfare of every man, woman, and child alive today.

The Perversion of Science

Luke 6:31 ESV

And as you wish that others would do to you, do so to them.

Psalm 52:2 ESV

Your tongue plots destruction, like a sharp razor, you worker of deceit.

The dirty secret about going green

Recently, a friend of mine was beaming as he described some of the features of his new home. In particular, he was proud of the expensive natural granite used for his countertops, windowsills, and front entryway. In his mind, selecting natural materials was a responsible, earth-friendly alternative to using man-made synthetic products. He was helping the earth, you see.

As his wife listened and smiled in smug admiration, I could see my own wife silently praying that I would not ruin a well-intended dinner invitation by speaking out on this subject. Unbeknownst to her, even without the prayer, I had already made up my mind not to comment on this subject. However, as fate would have it, my friend with scientific training only by way of CNN relentlessly baited me until I finally broke down and entered the conversation.

After explaining to him that while the granite was indeed itself a very eco-friendly material choice, it was perhaps more harmful to the environment and mankind than many man-made materials.

I explained that granite is extracted by digging and mining deep into the earth. The machines needed to mine, lift, cut, polish, and transport the heavy material all burn fossil fuels.

I added that when you consider that much of the fancier granite comes from places like Malaysia, one quickly realizes that the transportation of the beautiful but ultra-heavy granite consumes even greater amounts of fossil fuels to be shipped such great distances.

I further shared with him that there are many examples where the digging and mining for granite have devastated beautiful lands and precious water supplies.

Piling on the details, I pointed out that to keep oils, food, and other debris from ruining his granite, he would have to regularly apply chemical sealers, some of them not environmentally or people-friendly. When I added that those granite preservatives and cleaners were also carbon based and come from oil, he started to turn green; no pun intended.

Since he asked, I added that beautiful, elegant countertops made of recycled paper, glass (Terrazzo), and plastic were much more eco-friendly than granite and that wood and concrete were both highly durable materials as well.

Fortunately, my friend took it all in his stride and to my knowledge, was never angered by our conversation. My points are threefold.

1. If we are going to have scientific debates about the planet, we cannot just consider the information that supports our opinion on an issue. We must examine the entire picture.

2. Man cannot improve upon the efficiency of God's resources. Without exception for every attempt at modifying nature, the unsuspected negative effects are often tenfold worse.

3. Regarding our technologies and manufacturing, there is no such thing as permanent, planet-threatening activity. Regardless of the processes man chooses every ingredient we use in energy conversion is natural to the earth.

God and science both promise us an indestructible, self-sustaining planet.[31]

Moving forward, let us touch on a few more of the hypocrisies that the earth-saving perversionist would like us to believe.

Hybrid and electric vehicles

Hybrid vehicles are contraptions that consume both fossil and electric fuel. On the sole basis of technology, I think hybrid vehicles are interesting. Hybrid technology has been around for a long time, and the military has employed it for years. If you have a hybrid car, God bless you. Enjoy it. However, if you believe that owning a hybrid vehicle somehow makes you a friend of the earth and a better citizen, think again. As for electric cars, ditto.

These clean vehicles (CV) use either lithium ion or nickel-metal hydride batteries. They also require rare earth elements. As is the case with solar panels, these metals/minerals must be mined with fossil fuel-burning bulldozers and heavy handling/transportation equipment. The mining destroys the earth and the toxic chemicals used in metal refining drastically change the pH of nearby waters, often destroying fish populations.

Building a gas engine car produces 5.6 tons of carbon dioxide. Conversely, manufacturing one of these "green" electric or hybrid cars produces 8.8 tons of carbon dioxide.[32]

While a CV will produce less carbon dioxide over its lifespan, considering the higher production of carbon dioxide produced in its manufacturing, the actual net difference between a gas-

---

31   https://www.mpg.de/990456/earths_atmosphere_cleaning#:~:text=The%20earth's%20atmosphere%20is%20less,than%20some%20researchers%20previously%20thought.&text=Hydroxyl%20radicals%20clean%20the%20air,such%20as%20climate%2Ddamaging%20methane.
32   https://www.rd.com/article/the-problem-with-hybrid-cars/.

burning automobile and a CV is zero. The dirty little secret that the perversionist doesn't want us to know of course is that the production of these so-called clean vehicles consumes precious metals and creates devastating amounts of toxic pollution.

Once again, the attack on God manifests itself in the belief that his resources are bad for us.

Again, if you purchased a CV, God bless you. You gave someone a job, but you didn't do squat for the planet. If you purchased an electric contraption honestly thinking that you were helping the planet, then in essence you called God incompetent.

As a commentary on the silliness of the frantic push to drive a CV, Elon Musk, the most famous purveyor of the electric car, stated that the world is not even close to having enough electricity to charge these vehicles should people start accepting them universally.[33]

Let us take note that most of the electricity used to charge these "magic" clean vehicles comes from very fossil fuel-burning plants.[34]

Do you see the irony here? Without realizing it the perversionist has bowed his knee to God for even his own favored technology depends on the natural resources God has provided.

As always, I am not condemning the new technology of CVs. Clearly, they have a place in our world, and the individual who designed them received their talents from God. Clearly, God wants us to have CVs. It is the insistence that these new technologies are saving the planet and doing something God did not do for us that is the perversion.

---

33   https://medium.com/innomobility/its-hard-to-provide-enough-electricity-when-all-cars-are-electric-2d1447811455.
34   https://www.theguardian.com/environment/2016/dec/08/electric-car-emissions-climate-change.

The Perversion of Science

<u>Ecclesiastes 1:9</u>

What has been is what will be, and what is done is what will be done, and there is nothing new under the sun.

<u>Hydraulic fracturing – "fracking"</u>

I believe that only those stricken by a coma have not heard or read about the energy technology called hydraulic fracturing, or as it is commonly referred, fracking. It is a process whereby a solution of water and other ingredients such as sand and chemicals are injected underground at high pressure. The process causes small fractures in underground rock formations, which in turn allow shale oil and other previously trapped fossil fuels to escape and be harvested for use.[35] Fracking is not a new technology, and my school memory tells me that it was first used back in the 1940s. However, the popularity and application of fracking technology have grown exponentially over the past decade.

Along with this growth has come a heated battle between proponents who point to the new jobs and energy independence offered by the technology versus environmentalists who point to the potential damage to the environment.

Both scientifically and scripturally, fracking presents man with a conundrum. The Bible certainly advocates man investing and making a profit. It also describes to us the beauty of God's bounty, encouraging us to use and enjoy the fruits of the land. But we also cannot forget that God has commanded us to be good stewards of his Creation. Perplexingly, fracking involves all these issues. It provides great economic opportunity; it makes use of God's

---

35   https://www.americanrivers.org/threats-solutions/energy-development/fracking/?gclid=Cj0KCQiAoY-PBhCNARIsABcz773yJapdBEEbm2Q9rjHb-zZSU0-X3aFrykftU0T4mop17ZtY-JHBSVD0aAqvlEALw_wcB.

beautiful bounty, and then, as if to throw us a curveball, it presents undesirable, and sometimes unpredictable effects on the planet.

The topic of fracking is a unique phenomenon in the battle of God commanding us to use his abundance to make our lives better versus the perversionist who wants to cancel any process of energy that comes from nature.

Roughly 50 percent of our domestic oil supply comes from the fracking process. This oil is inexpensive to extract so from that aspect it is good for mankind. On the flip side, fracking does present great risks of poisoning our water and air.[36]

Some communities have reported methane coming out of their water faucets, and in many instances, it could be ignited. Fracking can pollute lakes and streams, displace wildlife with construction, and disturb otherwise isolated wilderness by turning it into industrial zones.[37] No energy conversion technology should harm people in this manner. This is not the way God wants us to use the bounty he has given us.

Man has tremendously minimized the downsides of conventional oil well drilling to where often, reasonably soon after the oil field has been depleted, there are no signs that drilling had ever occurred, and the land is returned to its previous condition. Unfortunately, this is not the current situation with fracking.

In my opinion fracking stands as an embarrassment to us in the way we fail to protect the associated environment. The good news is

---

36	https://money.cnn.com/2016/03/24/investing/fracking-shale-oil-boom/index.html.
37	https://www.americanrivers.org/threats-solutions/energy-development/fracking/?gclid=CjwKCAiA9tyQBhAIEiwA6tdCrFnD-Jy_Pb-4fWjUG1f24dc2tQa7TXrS-m_e5hv4MUAj3DCWigRa78Ro-CY2gQAvD_BwE.

that the technology that can make fracking safer and less disruptive already exists and stands right at our fingertips for the taking. I am going to go out on a limb and guess that the reason fracking is not more environmentally friendly is that the companies involved consider the costs too prohibitive to profitability.

The situation around fracking serves as a strong fortification of both our toolbox and my pushback on scientific perversion. What we can see here foremost is that regardless of the technology we consider, we must remain consistent in our assessments. Even if our assessment goes against our own agenda. Sometimes when we are honest and diligent in our assessments, we may find that we have common ground with our opponent.

In the case of fracking, those who pervert science attack this process largely to condemn God's gift of fossil fuels. This is wrong, it is evil, and we should never agree with it. However, the attack on fracking based on negative environmental and local economic impacts is indeed justified.

Jeremiah 2:7

And I brought you into a plentiful land to enjoy its fruits and its good things. But when you came in you defiled my land and made my heritage an abomination.

1 Corinthians 4:2

Moreover, it is required of stewards that they be found trustworthy.

Chapter Four

Anthropogenic Climate Change – Global Warming

Since 2006 the public awareness of global warming, now called climate change, has grown to become a daily talking point. First seeded by the documentary *An Inconvenient Truth*,[38] then promoted and supported without challenge in our media, the belief that man, through the normal consumption of our natural resources is destroying the earth and drastically modifying its climate has been accepted by many as fact. Nothing could be further from the truth, and when it comes to an apocalyptic hoax blossoming out of control, the theory of man-made global warming dwarfs the fictional scare created by the now-infamous Orson Wells radio presentation of *War of the Worlds*. Like Wells's presentation, Gore's "truth" is also pure science fiction.

One of the issues that bothers me, and it should bother you as well, is that the media and our government are doing everything they can to squash any voice, person or study that doesn't agree with the campaign to reduce our use of fossil fuels and substitute what is being scammed to us as new, clean, renewable technologies. Never in our history has the media and government controlled what scientific information the public is allowed to hear. Have we grown so complacent and lacking in character that we are afraid of contrary thinking? Have we lost the wisdom to cherish and seek

---

38   https://www.google.com/search?q=an+inconvenient+truth&oq=an+inconvenient&aqs=chrome.0.0i355i433i512j46i433i512j69i57j46i512l3j0i512l2j46i512j0i512.7612j0j7&sourceid=chrome&ie=UTF-8.

The Perversion of Science

it out?

Just as men squashed the truth from the lips of Jesus, so too today do they squash the truth of his science, the science that explains his promise of sustainability and abundance to us.

If we go to the library and use the Dewey Decimal System, we can find spectacular academic textbooks and research that contradict mainstream apocalyptic talking points. However, if we go to Google those same results will be suppressed and placed so far down in the search order that we would never know them to exist.

This is the sickness that fuels the proponents of climate change, and accordingly their attack on our faith.

On many levels, as you will see, the concept of man-made climate change is a physical impossibility. It not only violates the laws of science and nature, but also the laws of God. The concept of climate change has been positioned as a new protocol for how the media and government can achieve personal, economic, social, and political agendas.

By now, those non-believers and supporters of scientific perversion who are still reading along with us are experiencing their scientific world being turned upside down. On the one hand they cannot discount me as a religious fanatic, because scientific law also supports my scriptural positions. On the other hand, they are also coming to find out that their own apocalyptic beliefs have no secular and/or scientific standing.

Once again, before pummeling the misguided with facts, let us establish a solid foundation for this chapter by first considering some applicable Scripture, which in this case, exposes global climate change as fraud.

<u>Psalm 104:5</u>

He set the earth on its foundations so that it should never be moved.

<u>Ecclesiastes 1:4</u>

A generation goes, a generation comes, but the earth remains forever.

Now let's see how it all comes together with science.

The first major earthly flaw in climate change theory is that it violates the known medical and physical behavior of the human body. Perversionists want us to believe that our increased emissions of carbon dioxide, caused by the increased burning of fossil fuels, are so pronounced that they are wreaking havoc on the environment. If that is the case, then science also dictates that we should be witnessing additional phenomena known to be caused by CO_2.

Science has repeatedly shown that the human body begins to fail and struggle as carbon dioxide levels rise.[39] We all know that carbon dioxide is so toxic to humans that even slight increases in its concentration cause our heart rate and respiration to rise. Therefore, patients who undergo surgery have both their oxygen and carbon dioxide levels monitored by an anesthesiologist and respiratory therapist. It also explains why divers and astronauts have very precise instrumentation measuring the gas content in the air they breathe.

With that said, don't you find it bizarre, even cartoonish, that some unscrupulous scientists want us to believe that there is enough carbon dioxide to kill our planet, poison our oceans, and destroy plant and animal life, but not enough to influence our breathing, <u>which by the</u> way is a lot more sensitive to changes in carbon

[39] https://www.google.com/search?q=an+inconvenient+truth&oq=an+inconvenient&aqs.

dioxide than our planet?

Science tells us that athletes will perform at a decreased level if they are breathing in higher levels of carbon dioxide, but there is no evidence of this happening. How could so many new world records have been set at the recent Olympics if athletes were breathing in less oxygen and more carbon dioxide?[40]

Furthermore, the internal combustion engines in our cars, planes, and industrial equipment burn less efficiently as carbon dioxide increases and oxygen content decreases.[41] If carbon dioxide levels were increasing, our cars would be stuttering, going slower and losing horsepower. Our aircraft would have serious flight problems too horrific to fathom.

The chemical, pharmaceutical and electronics industries that rely on precise concentrations of gas in their manufacturing would likewise be experiencing negative effects and being forced to make process changes. But none of that is happening.

There's more. Fire extinguishers commonly use carbon dioxide as their active ingredient. Why is that? It is because science shows us that fires cannot thrive in increased carbon dioxide levels as it displaces oxygen, which is required for anything to burn.[42] So,

40   =chrome.0.0i355i433i512j46i433i512j69i57j46i512l3j0i512l-2j46i512j0i512.7612j0j7&sourceid=chrome&ie=UTF-8 nt%20or%20endurance%20athletic%20performance.&text=The%20low%20CO2%20responders%20recorded,than%20the%20high%20CO2%20responders.

41   https://www.ncbi.nlm.nih.gov/pmc/articles/PMC1332295/#:~:text=There%20has%20been%20some%20evidence,sprint%20or%20endurance%20athletic%20performance.&text=The%20low%20CO2%20responders%20recorded,than%20the%20high%20CO2%20responders.

42   https://www.sc.edu/ehs/training/Fire/05_co2.htm#:~:text=-Carbon%20dioxide%20extinguishes%20work%20by,cools%20the%20

one must ask, why is it that firefighters are not reporting an easier time putting out fires? Surely carbon dioxide levels high enough to change the entire climate of the earth, acidify the oceans, and destroy polar ice and coral reefs, would have some measurable effect on forest and field fires? But once again, this part of science, because it is truly inconvenient for the climate perversionist, is purposely, and in my opinion, criminally hidden from public conversation.

The next major flaw in warming theory has to do with atmospheric/barometric pressure and another irrefutable, fundamental law of science called Boyle's law.[43] Boyle's law can be expressed as follows.

$PV = k$

P is the pressure of a gas
V is the volume of the gas
k is a constant.

Boyle's law teaches us that the pressure and volume of gases are inversely proportional; that is to say if the pressure caused by a gas doubles, then the volume of that gas must be reduced by half.

Boyle's law can also be represented this way:

$P_1 V_1 = P_2 V_2$

$P_1 V_1$ = The initial pressure and volume of the gas
$P_2 V_2$ = The new, altered pressure and volume of gas
In this representation we see that as we change either the pressure or volume of a gas, the other component of the equation must also change in an exact, inversely proportional manner to maintain the constant.

---

fuel%20as%20well.
43   https://www.grc.nasa.gov/www/k-12/airplane/boyle.html.

The Perversion of Science

What proof do we have of an increase in carbon dioxide in our atmosphere?

If we accept the claims of perversionists that a dangerous amount (volume) of carbon dioxide is escaping and is trapped in our atmosphere, Boyle's law would demand an inversely proportional drop in barometric/atmospheric pressure readings of other gasses. But this isn't happening; there have been no credible findings that the world's atmospheric pressure is increasing due to this supposed claim of increased carbon dioxide. Again, we see how scientific laws expose the man-made climate change hoax.

Even if we put Boyle aside, our simple, common-sense understanding of gasses earmarks carbon dioxide-based climate change as horse sense.

The word *inflate* means to puff up, to fill an object with air or other gas. When we inflate an object one of only two things can happen.

1. The object expands and gets bigger – like a balloon
2. The object does not expand, and the internal pressure rises – like a tire

And so it goes too with our atmosphere that if man is increasing the amount of CO_2 being put into it, either the pressure must go up, or the size of the atmosphere must increase. There is no debate here. To my knowledge, the "experts," including NASA have not reported such phenomena. Since this science contradicts their perversion, we will not likely see them address this either.

Another known effect of carbon dioxide that climate perversionists conveniently sidestep is the fact that increased levels of carbon dioxide increase the rate at which plants grow. It is a well-known fact that greenhouse owners often mechanically increase the carbon dioxide environment to stimulate plant growth and reproduction.

According to the laws of science, if we increase the amount of carbon dioxide in our air and water, we should also experience an increase in the amount of plant life on both land and sea, which by the way would increase the rate at which the earth cleans and cools itself. Also, since plants produce oxygen, more plants would also mean cleaner air.

Do you see the conundrum here? If we produce more carbon dioxide, God's plants will multiply and consume it. So again, science tells us that man cannot affect the climate, but the "experts" among us just cannot seem to make up their minds.

NASA claims we are seeing more plant growth.[44] Conversely, the UN claims that climate change is increasing pests and causing plant life to decrease.[45] NASA also claims that increased carbon dioxide is producing more oxygen.[46] In 1971 NASA climate researcher Stephen Schneider predicted that an ice age was coming.[47] The climate on Mars is also warming, so somebody needs to tell those pesky Martians to stop burning fossil fuels.[48]

Years ago, comedian Kevin Nealon did a few Saturday Night Live Weekend Updates where every fifteen seconds he would contradict himself, stop dead in his monologue and say, "Forget about what I said earlier, I was just rambling, but this is what I really mean." If you read enough of those who are predicting environmental

---

44   https://climate.nasa.gov/news/2436/co2-is-making-earth-greenerfor-now/#:~:text=Studies%20have%20shown%20that%20increased,chief%20culprit%20of%20climate%20change.
45   https://news.un.org/en/story/2019/12/1052591.
46   https://www.nasa.gov/sites/default/files/atoms/files/making_o2_and_co2.pdf.
47   https://www.newscientist.com/article/dn11643-climate-myths-they-predicted-global-cooling-in-the-1970s/.
48   https://www.sciencefocus.com/space/is-mars-really-heating-up-quicker-than-earth/.

apocalypses, you will see that like Nealon's comedy, they too contradict themselves and change their story, often in the same presentation.

Another major flaw with warming theory is that the sample size used to make climate predictions is not scientifically valid. Remember that the perversionist stands boldly on his climate claims based on roughly one hundred years of data gathering. While he uses these sample numbers to impress the public, when held to true scientific methodology, he is left holding an empty bag because in addition to taking this one-hundred-year sample, the perversionist also maintains that the earth is 4.5 billion years old. Combining these two pieces of his own information absolutely crumbles the scientific foundation of global warming. Once again let's proceed according to proper scientific protocol prescribed by our toolbox.

Given:

Claimed age of earth: *4.5 billion years*

Climate change observation sample size   *100 years*

Based on this given information, simple division shows us that according to their gibberish, the earth has gone through forty-five million distinct, separate periods each comprised of one hundred individual years. Can you now see the flaw in the assumptions of climate change study? Let us highlight it in red for all to see!

The use of a single one-hundred-year grouping of temperature measurement data means that the climatologist is ignoring the other 449,999,999 samples available for study that they claim exist. So, what we are left with is climate theory based on only a 0.00000000222 fraction (1/45 million) of the total available data.

Please enlighten me. How can a study that only considers one forty-five-millionth of the data be accurate?

If your conclusion is that climate change theory is absurd and misleading, your perception would be correct.

There are two important points here: (1) everything I make claim to comes from laws. God's laws and the laws of science. (2) I am perfectly able to defend my positions in any academic debate and can stand firm on everything I what written and claimed.

The climate perversionist insists that God's planet is failing, yet his claims cannot stand the scrutiny of his own foundations.

Remember, it is not me who claims the earth is forty-five million years old. It is the blasphemer. He claims it, so he must stand by it and own it. I promise you, every one of these vile attacks on God's promise will be exposed as lies and fraud.

To put this perversion of science into a tangible example, I ask you, would you let a loved one take a new drug if you found out that in the process of testing the new product, the manufacturer only looked at one single test result out of a possible forty-five million? Of course, you would not, but you see that is exactly what these climate change perversionists are asking us to do. They are basing predictions of the earth's future using only one sample out of a possible forty-five million.

There is no research, laboratory or any other analytical convention known to man that would give scientific credibility to any study that only considered one of forty-five million possible samples. Even if the earth is only a few thousand years old, the sample size of climatology data is still invalid.

To make these fictional warming / climate change fantasies look even more idiotic, we must realize that some of the warming /

climate change predictions have focused on an even smaller sample size, often using a sample period of only ten years.

Oddly, those who are promoting climate change theory will not deny any of my points about sample size but will instead skirt the truth by citing technical nonsense about how their complex mathematical models have taken these variables into consideration and have made the proper adjustments to correct possible errors in sample size. This argument also is pure hogwash.

Mathematics cannot correct the unknown and unreliable data from the past and magically transform it into data that accurately blends into twenty-first-century technology.

What I dislike the most about theoretical climatologists is that they hide behind the future and never have to face scrutiny in the here and now. Every prediction they make is free of the burden of being proven today. They are like the schoolyard brat who because he is the one who brought the football to school changes the rules of the ballgame whenever they don't favor him.

When the actual current-day climate conflicts with the climate-change huckster's theoretical buffoonery, he simply switches to a new, modified theory and explains how his original findings were still accurate but simply needed to be updated.

Conversely, I don't have to waffle on God. Through volcanoes, tornadoes, hurricanes, drought, floods, fires, war, and nuclear bombs God's promises remain steadfast, and the earth keeps on renewing itself.

My sentiments about those who attack God by perverting science are succinct and clear. I see these men as vipers, as evil minions of Satan who cleverly omit, disguise, and twist any observations that contradict the self-loathing and pestilence they are trying to sell us. The Bible uses different words but expresses the same condemnation of the perversionist.

1 John 4:1 ESV

Beloved, do not believe every spirit, but test the spirits to see whether they are from God, for many false prophets have gone out into the world.

I think it speaks volumes about just how shaky global warming theory is that climatologists have minimized the term "global warming" and changed their discussions to the less aggressive, friendlier sounding term "climate change." I promise you, in the coming few years as the earth regulates itself as it always does, and as Mother Nature disobeys all the apocalyptic predictions, we will witness the climatologist again try to remain relevant by coming up with new, altered theories about the earth's climate. I promise you as the doom and gloom of climatology falls by the wayside, the perversionist will claim the earth's self-regulating properties are abnormal and they will try to explain how this too is part of their theory of a failing earth.

Man has not been recording temperature long enough to make any credible predictions one way or another about where our climate is headed.

I predict that soon perversionists will invent the phrase "global climate management." Oops, I just invented it. Kidding aside, if you remain attentive you will see the climatologist invent new jargon to insist that more than ever the future of the planet is in his hands.

Moving forward, yet another thunderously fatal flaw incorporated in climate change theory is the total lack of standardization of the temperature data that is being used. The chapter 1 toolbox example we studied about weight measurement demonstrated that scientific analysis has no validity unless from the beginning of the study, there is a purposeful standardization of both the instruments used and the way the data was collected.

It is crucial to recognize that the data warming theorists are commonly quoting is expressed in increments of one-tenth or even one one-hundredth of a degree. The outrage here is that there were no digital thermometers in 1900, and there was no available process to enable technicians of the day to record temperatures with such exact specifications. To reiterate, the accuracy of any study cannot exceed the accuracy of the instruments and process used to make the recordings.

Temperature measurement instrumentation back in 1900 through about 1980 was predominantly analog technology. The shortcoming of this older technology was not only its limited accuracy, but perhaps more importantly, its requirement that an observer visually "read" the instrument. The measuring process in those days presented a high degree of variability and potential human error. The instruments of even twenty-five years ago were not capable of satisfying the accuracy requirements of the mathematical climate models that perversionists are using to perpetuate climatology and CO_2 fraud.

The reason that these older instruments cannot be considered accurate as temperature recordings is that they were vulnerable to variability presented by eyesight, perspective, and parallax.

Eyesight is a very simple variable to understand. The vision of different individuals can vary dramatically and since reading thermometers in the early days relied on eyesight, it is only logical to conclude that early temperature readings were as inconsistent as the eyesight of the individual recording the observation.

Perspective is also a very simple variable to understand. Depending on the height, position and distance of the person recording data, the actual temperature recorded was subject to tremendous inaccuracy. Imagine that you are a passenger in an automobile that has a needle-type speedometer with a circular miles-per-hour scale. If you were to record the speed of the car from a normal passenger position, you would record that the car was going much slower than it was because your position would artificially skew the relationship of the needle with respect to the miles-per-hour markings. However, as you leaned to the left and viewed the speedometer straight on, you would record a much more accurate speed. In temperature measurements, the height and angle of the observer would have a direct effect on the perceived thermometer reading.

Parallax, as this is called, is the discrepancy of an object's actual position when it is looked at from two different lines of vision.49

As a simple demonstration close one eye, pick out an object on a wall in front of you, and hold your thumb up in front of your eye until that object is covered by your thumb. Next, without moving your head or your thumb, open your closed eye and close your opened eye. Upon doing this it will appear as if both your thumb and the object have moved in relationship to each other. The phenomena just listed affect all visual observations, and that most certainly affected early temperature measurements.

You might even want to try an experiment yourself. Put a mechanical (mercury) thermometer on a wall, inside or outside. Next have multiple people of varying heights read the thermometer and record their reading. Ask them to record the temperature to what they believe to be the nearest tenth of a degree. After everyone has written down their reading, examine all of them. You will be

49   https://www.merriam-webster.com/dictionary/parallax.

amazed to see how much variance there will be in recordings.

These inaccuracies and inconsistencies can also be experienced by repeating this entire process only this time mounting the thermometer a foot higher or lower. If the participants don't know why they are being asked to record their thermometer readings, and if you don't share the results with them from either experiment, you will come to discover that most, if not all the individual participants, will have recorded a different temperature for all the different readings.

These variances are a natural part of reading any analog measurement equipment and shouldn't be perceived as deception. However, if climatologists were ethical, they would acknowledge the great limitations of their hobby and their data. If we are being honest, according to basic analytical and academic standards, to claim scientific validity based on such flexible temperature data really is a perversion.

Another factor warming climatologists don't want you to know is that the locations and physical conditions of temperature measurement recorded over time have been as varied and inconsistent as the mind can imagine. Our modern cities have dramatically increased the amount of reflective concrete and vehicle heat compared to what they had in days gone by. These variables only add to the unscientific nature of climate change studies.

In addition, understand that there is no unbiased, pre-engineered scientific tool to standardize and homogenize randomly gathered temperature data from the past. Because of this, the climatologist has the freedom to manipulate and condition the data so that it best fits his individual mathematical model and personal agenda. This violates scientific protocol. For any scientific study to be valid, the individual performing that study cannot manipulate the data.

With climate change prognostications, the perversionist doesn't just manipulate data, but selectively eliminates or hides from public view any information that doesn't suit his purpose.

A final component of inaccurate historical temperature measurement can be attributed to normal human behavior. There has always been a light-hearted, competitive tendency to engage in "my dad is stronger than your dad" type shenanigans when it comes to reporting temperature. On any given day, when someone tells us how hot or cold their city is, who among us has not been tempted to win the debate and outdo their temperature reading by one tiny degree? Global climatologists can object all they want to my disrespectful take on their sacred science, but I can assure you that before the days of great mega-dollar global warming government grant giveaways, the entire science of temperature recording was a casual, laid-back process. In many cases it was even lackadaisical, and often it was anecdotal. There are so many holes in the potential accuracy of temperature measurement data that climate change theory must be considered fodder for the lover of fiction.

If there was no truth in my words, then my critics should be able to explain to me why, even as I write this book, there is still no accepted, standardized, universally agreed-upon convention for how global temperature is measured.

The reason for this is clear: if temperature measurements were standardized, there would no longer be wiggle room to manipulate data and fabricate mathematical models to support predetermined results.

The bad news for the believer in climate change theory doesn't end just yet. The laws of climate and weather protect us emphatically from a warming planet.

The Perversion of Science

Imagine for a moment that the earth was indeed warming. Science tells us that heat causes evaporation and evaporation causes rain. We all know that rain cools the earth. So, if the earth started to warm, it would experience higher evaporation rates and a subsequent increase in rains.[50] Increased rain would cool the planet and logically there could be no global warming. This process, put in place by God since the beginning of time will continue until the end of our time.

To show you just how perverted science has become, there is a PDF file on the blog post (footnote 50), in which the EPA confirms 100 percent what I have just said, but then, to appease their climate change financiers, go on to explain that even though the earth will indeed cool itself naturally, because of wind currents some geographic areas may be cooler than others, and some may be wetter than others.

Wow! That explains it to us. Now we know why it is hot in California and freezing in Antarctica. It is not nature, it is not the sun, it is not the position of the earth and the axis of rotation, but it is climate change that causes the climate to vary in different geographical areas.

I guess that we just didn't realize that before man began manufacturing and developing the planet, all geographic locations had the same identical temperature and precipitation. It was climate change that messed all that up!

Please understand, I am not condemning anyone who wants to study the theory of global warming, the environment, or climate change. However, I am condemning the scientifically fraudulent way the study is being conducted and forced down the throats of

---

50   https://wateristhenewgold.com/epa-contradicts-anthropogenic-climate-change-then-hedges/.

an unsuspecting public. I am condemning the Al Gore mentality that suggests man is destroying the planet.

If scientists want to study man-made global warming, then before making any predictions they must first ethically initiate the foundation for this study by creating a current-day, universally accepted, and standardized temperature measurement protocol.

Then, and only then, can man even begin to accumulate valid global temperature data. The information we have up until today for the purpose of long-term predictions is random and of little use in helping us understand our climate.

Supporters of climate change frequently boast that most climatologists agree that man is changing the earth's climate. Even if this consensus true, it has absolutely no bearing on the validity of man-made climate change. Science is not driven by majority support. In the world of science, majority thinking has been wrong perhaps even more than it has been correct.

"Mr. Columbus, you will fall off the end of the earth."
"DDT is safe."
"Asbestos is safe."
"Cigarettes are safe and non-addictive."
"If you get the COVID vaccine, you will be immune."

Since our government and their climate czars only make grant money available for scientists who support man-made climate change, and since the media only gives airtime to warming supporters, many researchers, in their quests to eat, pay their bills, and have favorable access to the media, behave as bobblehead dolls and unanimously support this economically destructive, immoral, and anti-Christian climate agenda.

I promise you, if the government suddenly made available $400 million for research into global cooling, you would find large numbers of these same researchers flip-flopping, switching teams, and lining up to convince us the earth is cooling.

Another dirty little secret that climate-change perversionists don't want you to know is that during our normal fluctuation in global temperature, other entities related to our solar system are also going through the same exact trends. Again, a simple Google search will show that temperatures on the surface of the sun, and on planets like Mars and our moon, have also shown parallel temperature changes, some of them even more severe than those on earth. I guess the aliens are burning too many fossil fuels?[51]

Authentic scientists know that it is the activity of the sun that ultimately heats earth and the rest of the solar system. In the citation just listed, these authors accept that the sun is responsible for warming our neighboring planets, magically not responsible for warming earth.

The final, fatal problem with climate-change theory is that its supporters routinely exploit technology to over-sensationalize their absurd positions. Facilitated by eye-in-the-sky telescopes, digital, on-location cell phone recordings, powerful photo enhancing/editing software and viral social media, the climate perversionist can create immediately villainous, evil, frightening images to convince the public that the latest storm is not only the worst ever, but also a hint of the devastation that is to come if we do not reverse our consumption of fossil fuels.

Nobody is more guilty of perverting science than NASA. Many if not most of the images NASA releases to the public are photoshopped, colorized and otherwise digitally enhanced. In

---

51   https://www.resonancescience.org/blog/Is-Our-Solar-System-Heating-Up.

essence those fantastic astronomical sights we see from NASA in the media are pretty much the same things we see in George Lucas films.

Until recently, NASA hid this tomfoolery very well in the fine print of the photo, but now that savvy viewers have caught on, NASA's official position is that they admit the photos are fake, but they are for the purpose of allowing scientists to better understand their findings.[52]

In other words, when NASA telescopes capture radio waves, they call in the kid from TikTok who makes cool monster illusions to make their "scientific" findings more believable.

NASA doesn't exist to help mankind. It exists to further the desire to prove that God doesn't exist and that there is nothing special about life on earth.

Today, storms serve as another tool that the enemies of God bludgeon us with in their effort to convince us that we are destroying earth. The pictures and videos of storms today have all the trappings of a Hollywood science-fiction film and are produced to generate unsubstantiated fear and guilt in the world.

In days gone by, we would learn about a storm in the paper or in a grainy video on television. It only makes sense that these modern, enhanced visuals of storms have a dramatic impact on us. I remember how much of the world was living in fear when the movie *The Exorcist* was released. That too was fiction.

Sadly, public information about the weather often has very little to do with science and everything to do with promoting personal, perverted agendas.

---

52   https://science.nasa.gov/all-these-space-images-are-fake-except-one.

Contributing to this self-serving over-sensationalizing of weather is the fact that just about everyone has a cell phone. In 1960 we were lucky to catch a few tornadoes on film in a year. Today, no tornado can touch down without being video captured by hundreds of wannabe social media influencers. The perversionist supports his apocalyptic claims by pointing to how many more storms we see today. The reality of this hoax global warming is that since 1945 hurricanes are down about one-third.[53] The findings are similar for tornadoes.

We must also understand that the amount of destruction a storm wreaks is not directly related to how severe it is. Storms that touch highly populated areas will logically do more damage than storms that stay out at sea. For example, Hurricane Sandy, which devastated the East Coast, was not a particularly severe storm. It was at its most severe in Cuba, at a Category 2, and then decreased to a Category 1 and then decreased to a tropical storm rating when it traversed the US East Coast. What made Sandy so destructive was that it hit densely populated areas.

Katrina was also devastating because it brushed up against highly populated areas, but more so because local government failed to provide safety and containment structures, and because masses of people ignored warnings to evacuate. It is amusing to witness the myopic and one-sided views of climate change perversionists. They would have us believe severe weather and climate change never happened before while doing everything in their power to hide accurate climate history.

It is important to remember that the world, especially the ocean coastline areas, are far more populated today than they were a few decades ago. It is only reasonable to have more damage and loss

[53]   https://rogerpielkejr.substack.com/p/a-remarkable-decline-in-landfalling.

now. But that is a population and real estate issue, and not one of God's earth coming apart at the seams.

Starring in the 1957 movie *Rainmaker*, Burt Lancaster portrayed climatology perversionist Bill Starbuck who claimed that he could heal the planet by bringing rain to end a horrible, life-threatening drought. This movie was, of course, fictionally based on the reality of the horrible drought that devastated the Great Plains and will forever be called *the Great Dustbowl*. This movie provides great lessons for all of us, regardless of personal views.

On the one hand, the Great Dustbowl tells us that even in recent history when fossil fuel usage was not an issue, the earth still threw violent, devastating weather at us. Furthermore, Lancaster's Starbuck demonstrates that the buffoonery culture of Al Gore claiming man must heal a sick planet is a sickness that has been with us for a long time.

Hidden in both the movie and in history is a very important lesson about climate, science, and God. It is a lesson worth taking to heart.

An important aspect of this movie is that even Hollywood documents the actual severity of our climate back then and illustrates the gift of self-regulation and self-propagation that God instilled in our planet.

It is also important to remember that the reason the Great Dustbowl was so devastating was that ten years prior to the drought, the earth bequeathed that area of the nation with bountiful, beautiful, enriching rains and fertile, seeding winds. Long before the infamous drought, the natural ever-changing climate of the earth made the Great Plains fertile, and it attracted many thousands to relocate and enjoy the fertile farming that resulted.

Can you imagine if Al Gore and his sidekick Michael Moore were active back then? For ten years they would have gotten rich by predicting the end of man due to global rain. Then when the drought came, they would have switched over to global drought.

Make no mistake, anyone who maintains that earth is in trouble and can only be saved by man is evil. Al Gore and his disciples are the quintessential, real-world representation of the fictional environmental huckster Bill Starbuck.

Here is what should really trouble us about this climate perversion. Since climate change is a theory and not a law, why is it that there is no time given to listening to the dissenting voices? If a supposed 97 percent of climatologists believe in climate change, why can't we be given a list of these people so we can see for ourselves who agrees and who doesn't?

As it was in the days of Jesus, and so too is it today, contrary ideas frighten charlatans, politicians and the hand puppets we call the media. Only the evil, the unscrupulous, the immoral cannot face truth.

If this oppression of contrary ideas is allowed to continue, perhaps one day soon our courts will be conducted with only one attorney representing only one point of view.

As we close this chapter, we need to pause and reflect that throughout time, all phenomena applicable to our environment, including climate and carbon dioxide levels have displayed ever-changing dynamics. There has never been a time when our climate has not changed, and there has never been an instance where any scientist could demonstrate why these changes happen or predict them.

Studies done in hindsight are not science; they are conjecture.

Conversely, Scripture tells us in many places that God gave us the earth and bountiful resources to use as we need. Scripture assures us that man can do nothing to hurt the earth and that it will remain for us. Science has never once conflicted with Scripture and Scripture has never once had to change because of science.

I cannot say this enough. Any man who claims that the earth is failing, or is inadequate in any way, is attacking God, and being driven unknowingly or otherwise by evil.

There is no such thing as global warming, we are not running out of resources, and the planet does not need our help to survive. The concert of both God and science closes this discussion with the crack of thunder.

Jeremiah 17:7–8

Blessed is the man who trusts in the Lord, whose trust is the Lord. He is like a tree planted by water, that sends out its roots by the stream, and does not fear when heat comes, for its leaves remain green, and is not anxious in the year of drought, for it does not cease to bear fruit.

Chapter Five

Big Bang Theory and Creationism

The big bang theory (BBT) is the most famous pagan explanation for how the universe and all life was created. It is a theory that maintains there was no God or Creator involved. Make no mistake, at the forefront of BBT is an undying hate for Christianity. It isn't a stretch to say that the overwhelming majority of BBT researchers are passionately driven to be the first to prove that there is no God, and the overwhelming majority of them are atheists and pagans.

Sadly, BBT has grown in popularity, and today it is widely held by the pop culture segment of the scientific community as the most plausible explanation for the origin of our existence.

However, upon close examination we find that BBT has two flawed fundamental concepts as its foundation. In my opinion these concepts are born of imbeciles.

The first BBT concept is that almost fourteen billion years ago, before there was any life, the only things that existed were time and space. Don't ask where the time and space came from because this is the fudge factor in which the BBT proponent will tell us that time and space always existed.

In any case, the theory goes on to state that the mass of time and space became so immensely heavy that it all collapsed onto a single point. It then became very hot and started to expand rapidly. After expanding, this mess began to cool. The cooling supposedly allowed energy to be converted into mass, specifically, subatomic particles, which would serve as the building blocks for all physical matter.

BBT then projects that thousands of years later the first complete atoms were formed. Supposedly, these atoms, the precursors of our existence, were hydrogen, helium and a wee bit of lithium thrown in for flavor. Some proponents also include methane, carbon dioxide, ammonia, and water into the mix. Proponents call this the primordial ooze or primordial soup.[54]

At yet a later date, the theory holds that these atoms joined together to form celestial-like clouds, and with the help of gravity formed the more complex elements, stars, and galaxies. From these formations, according to BBT, life eventually emerged. The theory maintains that all life, both plant and animal came from the same original cosmic egg/cell.[55]

The first time I heard about the BBT was in a college biology class in 1974. Back in those days, BBT was presented as a theory, just one possible way in which the earth and living things might have come to be. In those days, university classrooms still considered it plausible that both a Creator coupled with a major cosmic event could both be responsible for beginning life.

However, as academics ran into dead ends with their theories about the origin of earth, they became bitter and turned sharply against God. You see, for them to admit the need for a universal Creator, was to accept intellectual defeat, and even worse, perhaps accept an end to government grant money for their far-fetched research.

BBT was first popularized by Carl Sagan, famous both for his

---

54 https://www.dictionary.com/browse/primordial-soup.
55 http://www2.estrellamountain.edu/faculty/farabee/biobk/biobookcell1.html.

"billions and billions" jargon, and for his appearances in the media and university speaking tours.[56] I never found Sagan to be credible because his insistence that the universe came from nothing violated the law of conservation of mass, a law that on many other occasions he firmly stood on to make many of his other scientific proclamations.

Sagan understood scientific law very well; however, his willingness to gerrymander those laws as it suited his agenda led him to many blasphemous and ridiculous theories.

Much of what Sagan professed was not only ridiculed by the very scientific laws, subjects, and experiments that he studied, but many times, what he pompously professed as being novel and unique, had already been magnificently presented to us in Scripture centuries before.

Let us take a slight detour and look at just one example of where BBT actually plagiarizes and steals from Scripture.

Modern science has accurately discovered and documented that our universe is constantly expanding. Each celestial body in the universe is moving away from the other bodies. To briefly explain, we know this by the method of measuring the light spectrum that is emitted from celestial objects. When we measure light that is shifted away from the white spectrum and toward the red spectrum, we have learned that the object in question is moving away from the viewer. Edwin Hubble discovered this in 1929, and Sagan spoke of it often.

---

56   https://www.goodreads.com/quotes/7203486-if-the-general-picture-of-an-expanding-universe-and-a#:~:text=%E2%80%9CIf%20the%20general%20picture%20of%20an%20expanding%20universe%20and%20a,confront%20still%20more%20difficult%20questions.&text=In%20many%20cultures%20it%20is,the%20universe%20out%20of%20nothing.

This most certainly sounds like an impressive discovery, so why I am pooh-poohing the big bang / expanding universe stuff? Well, maybe because long before Hubble and Sagan, the Bible already told us that the universe was expanding?

Isaiah 40:22 ESV

It is he who sits above the circle of the earth, and its inhabitants are like grasshoppers, who stretches out the heavens like a curtain, and spreads them to dwell in.

Psalm 104:2

Covering yourself with light as with a garment, stretching out the heavens like a tent.

Debate it however you may, but the act of expanding the universe and stretching the universe are the same things. This knowledge came from God, not from man's scientific discovery.

And speaking of unexplained science, both BBT and the general theory of gravity claim that larger, more massive objects pull smaller objects toward them. If this is the case, how can the universe be expanding? Why is the universe not collapsing on itself now, but supposedly only did so during the big bang? Isn't it amazing how scientific principles magically change at the mere mention of God?

Also note that Sagan and the rest of our scientists do not know why the universe is expanding. They do not know if it will keep expanding, or if it merely expands and contracts as do our lungs when we breathe. The takeaway here is that once again, science cannot explain Creation.

Getting back to the mainstream discussion, BBT theory was always contradictory to Christianity, but Sagan was not the one who weaponized astronomical theory and started a war with

God. That strike of evil was initiated by the world-renowned, self-proclaimed, origin-of-existence expert Steven Hawking.[57] Hawking openly scoffed at the idea of God and his work truly marked the beginning of Satan perverting science to facilitate the demise of Christianity.

Some of the scientific research and discovery associated with the BBT and the search for our origin have been impressive, and new observations are being made seemingly with every tick of the clock.

Unfortunately, many of the conclusions drawn from these observations are skewed and questionable. Rational conversations about this theory have become impossible because the proponents are completely shut off from the logic of a Creator. As such, when comparing our beliefs to BBT we must step back and compare how each of these ways of thinking is supported and defended.

We Christians readily admit that the belief in our God as the Creator requires faith. Perversionists mock us for having such faith; however, our beliefs are consistent with the laws of God. There is no contradiction in our beliefs.

Conversely, as we are about to learn the BBT version of man's origin requires proponents to disregard the very laws of the science that they claim as their foundation. Even the BBT proponent contradicts BBT.

Understand the point here. Scripture provides a credible explanation

---

57   https://www.brain-sharper.com/science/stephen-hawking-big-bang/?utm_campaign=VV%3E10%20Peaceful%20Dogs%20Omry0812%20En%20-%20Pmax%20USA%20GA&utm_source=AdWords&utm_medium=&gclid=CjwKCAiA0KmPBhBqEiwA-JqKK464-1LgxhtsRXrDU4rTUtuJeXTaLw3S8-6RFCWo3lgjuWR7A-PushZBoCKcUQAvD_BwE.

of Creation, one that is not built upon contradictions. Creationism is consistent and plausible because the biblical word is supported by both scientific law and common sense.

Genesis 1:1

In the beginning God created the heavens and the earth.

If we eliminate emotion from this conversation, we will see that most of the conclusions scientists are drawing about new cosmic observations look very suspect.

Armed with formulae, equations, graphs, and as we learned earlier, copiously digitally altered Hubble Telescope images BBT scientists can viscerally stimulate our imaginations and create great excitement about the cosmic origins of our being. But their process is far closer to a George Lucas movie than it is to science. The BBT proponent relies completely on smoke and mirrors to make his points.

I want to take a sidebar here and acknowledge that I know I am spending a lot of effort dissecting BBT. However, it is crucial to understand that this is the battleground where Satan first realized that he could create powerful weapons against Christianity in the form of perverted science. All the scientific perversions outlined in the introduction and earlier pages were incubated in BBT.

Let us look at where BBT falls flat on its own back.

A huge and fatal flaw of BBT is that not one theorist can explain the origin of the ingredients for this big explosion. Let us be clear on how fatal this problem is.

Even if 100 percent of the observations, projections, calculations, and theories surrounding the big bang are true, even if all the claims about heating, expanding, and cooling are correct, the theory demands that we believe that all the crucial ingredients of Creation just happened to be floating around with no Creator and no origin. Can you say coocoo for Cocoa Puffs?

In the world of experimental/laboratory science, man can forge out complex chemistries from simple ones such as hydrogen, helium, and lithium. There is no debate or argument here because for centuries inventors have been developing new, complicated products from the simplest ingredients. That carpet polyester can be fabricated from antifreeze is certainly a miracle that chemistry, through God of course, has brought us.

In his misguided journey, however, the BBT perversionist points to man's ability to synthesize more complex elements from simple ones and then proclaims that this validates that the big bang also created more complex matter, even life from these original simple elements.

But where did the ingredients to make the hydrogen, helium and lithium come from? If not from God, where did these ingredients come from?

Any fool can make a cake if he is given the ingredients. However, I want to see the perversionist make his own ingredients. When he can make his own oxygen, lithium, hydrogen, and carbon then we can talk about BBT.

It is important at this point in the book that we all come to a unified and high position of clarity in our debate of BBT versus God, the Creator. This is the most vital point of the Creation debate, and as Christians, we must arm ourselves with this weapon and have it ready to fire.

When we ask the proponent of BBT where the primordial ingredients came from, when we cite scientific laws that show mass cannot be created from nothing, the perversionist tries to flip the logic on us and asks, "Then where did God come from?"

No, no, no! That question is not applicable to God. Christians have never once maintained that God obeys or can be explained by the laws of science. Quite the opposite, we have said all along that God is the Creator, and that he existed before the universe.

Conversely, it is the perversionist who is claiming that science proves the big bang. As such it is up to the perversionist to use his science and demonstrate to us that the big bang is authentic. Remember, faith is not mentioned anywhere in BBT journals. It is bound by the laws of science. If those laws betray the theory, the proponent does not get to shift his failures into a discussion of God.

Whether or not God exists has no bearing on discussions of the big bang theory. The only reason God is ever entered into this conversation is that in trying to scientifically validate the big bang theory the perversionist runs into a dead end and science fails him. When the perversionist cannot answer the question of "Where did the ingredients come from," unwittingly, he bends his knee and admits that there must be a God.

Now, he can refuse to use God's name, but know this, every scientist who believes in the big bang will end his defense of it by admitting that the ingredients had to come from somewhere. The only difference between the big bang proponent and the Christian is that we know and accept the One who created these things.

Continuing then, for BBT to be valid, and for creationism to be shown to be invalid, the perversionist must be able to recreate the spontaneous generation that he maintains was responsible for the universe.

Spontaneous generation is a phenomenon whereby something is

created out of the blue, all by itself, with no ingredients and no help from humans. We must remember here that one of the non-negotiable conditions of a scientific law is that the scientist must be readily able to repeat the phenomenon he is promoting. If the big bang happened once, science tells us that it must be repeatable.

As it turns out, nowhere in the history of man or science has there been a single recorded instance of spontaneous generation. Given this fact, BBT believers wear the same aluminum foil helmet as those who believe in Bigfoot, UFOs, and zombies.

Perversionists and non-believers would challenge that no one ever witnessed God creating something from nothing. This is true; however, Christians never claimed that man could repeat or witness Creation. The perversionist is the one claiming that they can repeat the creation of life. So, show us!

Speaking of spontaneous generation, we do have multiple accounts of it from different observers of the works of Jesus Christ. As we know, such things only happened by the hand of God.

2 Kings 4:42–44 ESV

A man came from Baal-shalishah, bringing the man of God bread of the first fruits, twenty loaves of barley and fresh ears of grain in his sack. And Elisha said, "Give to the men, that they may eat." But his servant said, "How can I set this before a hundred men?" So, he repeated, "Give them to the men, that they may eat, for thus says the Lord, 'They shall eat and have some left.'" So, he set it before them. And they ate and had some left, according to the word of the Lord.

John 2:9 ESV

When the master of the feast tasted the water now become wine, and did not know where it came from (though the servants who had drawn the water knew), the master of the feast called the bridegroom

So that we may stand our ground in these attacks on our God, be attentive to when the perversionist challenges the validity of Scripture based on our faith, scoffing that it requires believing in things that were written more than two thousand years ago, remind him that his BBT nonsense requires belief in things that are millions of years old and have no documented records or witnesses. Also remind him that BBT theory violates the very same laws of science that his education and degrees are founded in.

Another problem with BBT is that it contradicts itself with the modern-day discipline of astronomy and stellar equations. On the one hand the perversionist wants us to believe that the original primordial soup became so heavy that it collapsed on itself and then the energy and heat created caused an explosion, which then created life. However, they also maintain that when the super mass of a collapsing star converges on itself it does not explode and create life, but instead it keeps collapsing inward and forms an invisible cartoon concept that we know as a black hole. So, which is it? Does a huge mass collapse and explode into life, or does it keep collapsing into a black hole?

Both ideas are born of imbeciles, but even the imbecile will eventually realize that he can't contradict himself and be taken seriously.

If there is one consistent behavior with the perversionist it is that all his theories contain hedge factors, wiggle room, apologies, adjustments, and exceptions. Scripture on the other hand stands firm, flawlessly on its own.

Next up, another fatal flaw with BBT.

We learned in our toolbox that no reaction or process is ever 100 percent efficient. To refresh, there are always leftover, unused, unreacted ingredients that remain after any process. For instance, who has not smelled the ingredients of an apple pie long after it was baked and devoured, or the scent of sulfur after firecrackers have exploded? This is this exact natural law that enables forensic scientists to solve crimes long after they have been committed.

If an explosion the magnitude described by BBT did occur, it would have splattered un-reacted, unused remnants of the fabled primordial ooze all across the universe. If such an explosion occurred, we would have discovered traces of the ooze. Because this ooze was supposedly a precursor to life, it would be an ingredient unlike anything we have seen before and would stick out in nature like a sore thumb. As such, it would be easily detectable by scientific methodology.

Unfortunately, to the embarrassment of the perversionist, no such discovery has ever occurred.

- The earth has supposedly endured billions of years of cosmic collisions from the very ends of the universe, yet no crater, asteroid or meteor has ever been found to contain traces of primordial ooze.
- No sample from the moon, also subject to billions of years of collisions and debris, has ever been shown to have anything resembling primordial ooze.
- Depending on the professor or perversionist, we have supposedly been visited by aliens, but again, no primordial ooze is to be found anywhere they are reported to have been.
- Our returning spacecraft have never been contaminated with even a grain of primordial ooze.
- No scientific experiment to reproduce something that could

pass as primordial ooze has ever been successful.

- Big bang theorists cannot provide a chemical formula in theory to predict the ingredients of this *Star Trek* fantasy goop.

Scripture also delivers a blistering slap in the face to those who try to sidestep the primordial ooze issue.

<u>Hebrews 11:3 ESV</u>

By faith we understand that the universe was created by the word of God, so that what is seen was not made from things that are visible.

Imagine that I placed apples, butter, flour, sugar, milk and all the utensils required to make an apple pie onto my kitchen countertop next to my stove and then went out for the night. Do you imagine that when I returned home, I would open the door to find an apple pie waiting for me? Do you imagine that if I repeated this experiment a billion times I would ever come and find a properly baked apple pie waiting for me? Of course, not.

As absurd as a spontaneous apple pie strikes us, the idea of BBT is even more absurd because the huckster is asking us to believe that all of Creation came to be in this very exact ridiculous type of random event. Surely the possibility of a spontaneous apple pie is a more reasonable expectation than a spontaneous universe. So where is my apple pie?

Before we move on, at the risk of beating a dead horse, the second law of thermodynamics has yet one more punch to deliver to the BBT perversionist.

This law tells us that in any reaction all the particles involved will at some point lose all their energy and come to rest. This is also called the law of entropy.

Let's recall our early illustration of entropy. When we drop a bucket full of marbles on the floor they will first race off, scattering in all directions, bouncing off each other and anything they run into. However, at some point, they will all come to rest. At that point they are known to have discharged all their energy and can only move again if someone applies new force/energy to them.

Let us apply this to BBT.

If there was indeed a big bang, all the particles from that explosion would, by scientific law come to rest. However, that is not what happened.

The universe is in perpetual motion. We observe orbits and rotation of celestial objects, and we know that out in the universe, every star, planet and galaxy is constantly moving away from each other.

These motions defy BBT and the laws of known science. They can only be explained in supernatural terms. They can only be explained in terms of God and Scripture.

I would like to impart a final thought about BBT.

People normally study science because they are driven by a passion for helping others. Medical professionals heal the sick. Engineers build things and find ways to make life safer, faster, more enjoyable, and more economical. Chemists develop drugs, fuels, dyes, fertilizers, insecticides, water treatment chemicals, and they help virtually every product in our lives. Biologists help us to understand nature, find better ways to farm, and work with every imaginable living organism. These passions are a gift from God that we might live more fruitful, enjoyable lives.

A beautiful characteristic of authentic scientists is that they leave demonstrable proof that they were here. They leave us better off than they found us. The fruits of their work can be seen, smelled, touched, and tasted. I believe that the most important characteristic of a true scientist is that they leave us the notebook of how to reproduce their work.

Sadly, somewhere in the late '70s, we began to see a new breed of scientist, the theoretical scientist. This type of scientist, the worst perversionist of all, works on things that cannot be smelled, touched, tasted, and felt; things that cannot be proven. The theoretical scientist soils every good thing that gets in his way and sets himself up, with corporate or government funding, as the genius who will deliver the unanswered questions of the universe.

For the record, there is not one global warming scientist, not one notable proponent of evolution, green technology, or life on other planets, who is not funded by the government or a corporation. Additionally, there are no detractors of these things who are funded by the government or a corporation.

The BBT proponent is not driven by righteousness or a desire to help man, but instead by the desire to be recognized as an expert above God. This self-drunk scientist is a cancer to humanity and a driving force of the perversion I am writing about.

Chapter Six

NASA: A Real Global Threat

Some readers may find it shocking that I have included NASA in a book that explores the perversion of science and scientific attacks on Christianity, but please be attentive because NASA is indeed actively involved in both. I believe it is important for us to take a close look at how NASA affects the moral and ethical components of the world in which we live.

There are few things that Americans hold with higher respect than NASA. We adore NASA. We revere the brave men and women who travel into space. We stand in awe and elevate on pedestals the scientific NASA geniuses who constantly bring us new ideas and introduce us to exciting unknown theaters of science. Our passion for NASA and outer space is so intense that many times the blending of Hollywood screenwriting and science is so intertwined that we lose sight of where reality stops, and fantasy begins.

I maintain that NASA's strongest zealots believe that the organization is man's highest scientific authority and that it will one day prove there is no God. In that regard, NASA is unwittingly being implemented by many as a perverted weapon against Christians. It is my opinion that NASA has lost its direction and now serves only as a tool for Satan to attack our faith.

Fortunately, we can rejoice and take comfort because both science and Scripture bring this irresponsible, self-important monster back down to earth.

If we are to believe many of NASA's claims, then we are expected to accept that the earth is fragile, and the Creator is incompetent. I cannot stress enough how subtle but vicious these seemingly innocent agendas are against Christianity and mankind. Disguised in the cloak of "taking care of the planet" this dangerous weapon doesn't just attack our faith, but it also attacks any enthusiastic, young Christian scientific mind who might dare to differ with the mainstream agenda that the earth is endangered.

For these reasons, an honest critique of NASA is warranted.

When NASA was created in 1958 there was no mention of climate. The components of the mission statement focused on learning about space travel and building vehicles capable of transporting research materials into space. The specific purpose was to determine how learning about the universe/space could benefit mankind.[58] Note that in this mission statement was some casually flossed over language about sharing any information about weapons discoveries with the US government. To have even mentioned this in 1958, we see clearly that weaponizing space was a seed planted very early. Beneficial to mankind?

In the original Cape Canaveral days, NASA had the most noble goals. In those days, each new journey was filled with diverse purpose and carried with it the hope of improving our lives and serving humanity. In those days, NASA ached to find new medicines, chemicals, farming and manufacturing processes that could supposedly be only done in the new, recently reachable zero-gravity conditions of space.

In those days, NASA sought to learn how disease, bacteria, viruses,

---

58   https://history.nasa.gov/spaceact.html#:~:text=To%20provide%20for%20research%20into,atmosphere%2C%20and%20for%20other%20purposes.

and plants behaved away from earth and then apply what was learned to help humanity. In those days, NASA was an independent organization free of financial interference; it was not driven to support the agenda of a president or political agenda.

Sadly, today NASA has been reduced to burping up daily media propaganda, which insists that every new telescopic image is yet more proof that there are many other planets just like earth, that there is life on those planets, and that there once was life on celestial rock piles like Mars, Venus and, the now no-longer-a-planet, Pluto.

Sadly, another major portion of NASA's efforts is spent in yet another hoax, the hoax of global climate change.

In the glory days of NASA, scientists were not blinded from God by the pomp of new and exciting scientific journeys. In those days, NASA encouraged alternate and contrary research. In those days, the heroes, the fearless explorers who comprised NASA, universally recognized that all discoveries and observations obeyed both the laws of science and the laws of God. In my opinion NASA is now careening about with reckless abandon. The underlying focuses of NASA today, intended or not, serve to puff up man's pompous self-importance, ridicule Christianity, and by perverted celestial conclusions, insist that there is no God.

For those non-believers who find my comments to be more editorial than factual, let's talk a closer look at this subtle perversion. A couple of short quotes remind us of the nobility and wisdom that were an integral and foundational core of the original NASA.

"To look out at this kind of Creation and not believe in God is to me impossible."

– Astronaut John Glenn

"In the beginning, God created the heavens and the earth."

– Astronaut Frank Boorman, Apollo 8 commander speaking at 250,000 miles away from earth while orbiting the moon.

On December 24, 1968, the entire Apollo 8 crew took turns reciting Genesis 1: 1–10[59].

Am I insinuating that the faith of our magnificent former astronauts is proof positive that God exists? Let's look at it another way. The astronauts were all men of science. They studied countless hours, endured grueling mental and physical conditioning, and then were tested so that they could put into practice in space, the most critical scientific laws and principles known to man. Literally, their lives depended on a command of science. With all that said, these men believed in God and Jesus Christ. And it follows that they too believed God's promise of an indestructible earth, with endless abundance.

Perversionists like Al Gore, Michael Moore, Neil deGrasse Tyson, and Stephen Hawking, with the help of political agenda, however, have helped change the direction of NASA and draw it away from a spiritually sound foundation.

Perhaps the most prolific scientific perversion about NASA is the belief that every new and important technological advancement we have enjoyed over the past fifty years has come about because of our space program.

To be honest, many modern-day products such as memory foam, smoke detectors, scratch-resistant lenses and athletic shoe inserts did originate from ideas and applications within NASA. In addition, Hubble has allowed us to brace for severe weather, and in

---

59   http://rexcrum.wordpress.com/2013/12/24/in-the-beginning/.

so doing saved lives and property. These type of accomplishments are wholesome, and in line with what NASA was created for.

There are, however, many other NASA-credited technologies including cordless tools, certain water filtration technology, microcomputers, integrated circuits, cell phone technology and the Internet that were already well under development by the time NASA incorporated them into their work.

Other creations attributed to NASA, such as TANG had absolutely no connection other than they were existing products selected for NASA's use.

It is important that we keep a proper perspective on NASA and remember that men gifted by God are forever working on fantastic things with no help from any government agency. While NASA has facilitated grant/research money to perfect many technologies, even without NASA many of these things would still have come to be.

Konrad Zuse developed the first programmable computer in 1936.[60] Throughout the '40s and '50s, companies were making smaller and smaller computers for tasks such as reading checks, managing banking records and even picking presidential elections.

In January of 1956, a short story called "The Dying Night" was printed in a magazine called *Fantasy and Science Fiction*[61] in which its author, Isaac Asimov, spoke about minicomputers. Certainly, Apple and Windows/PC computers never went to the moon and were developed long after the road was paved by real genius.

In 1906, in a publication called *Punch Magazine*, Lewis Baumer

---

60   https://people.idsia.ch/~juergen/zuse.html.
61   *The Magazine of Fantasy and Science Fiction*, January 1954 (Vol 11, No. 1) ASIN B08QTZN1WH, Fantasy House.

published a cartoon that depicted people communicating remotely on wireless telephone technology.[62] Successful wireless telephone technology was being implemented as far back as 1918, some of it by the railroad industry.[63] Mobile cell phones were invented in the 1940s[64] and benefitted from forty-plus years of R&D before becoming available to the public in the late '80s.

In *Matthew 6:25–34*, when God tells us not to worry about what we will eat or wear, he wasn't just reassuring us about food and clothes. He was also reassuring us that he would provide our every necessity. When we worry about how we will be sustained tomorrow, we marginalize God and fail to see that in addition to the natural staples of our existence, he also blesses us with genius, inventiveness, and creativity to fortify his promise of abundance.

We don't need NASA for this. All that we need, in every seen and unseen manner has been accounted for by God.

One might ask why it matters if NASA is given credit for all these things. It matters on several levels. First, from a Christian perspective, this kind of thinking inflates egos to the point where, as you see today, man starts believing that only he has authority and power in the areas of his own origin and destiny. This kind of thinking steers us away from God and marginalizes the precious spiritual camaraderie alluded to by the astronauts just quoted. From a scientific perspective, this kind of thinking distracts from the orthodox pursuit of science and original thought. It leaves future students with a conditioned belief that engaging in a life of science

---

62 https://relevantmagazine.com/culture/1906-cartoon-predicted-smart-phone/.
63 http://www.trainweb.org/oldtimetrains/CNR/cgr/mobile_phone_1918.htm.
64 https://www.uswitch.com/mobiles/guides/history-of-mobile-phones/.

carries with it the moral mandate to work only within the most current, popular, and mainstream scientific trends.

That our media is completely devoid of any scientific opinion and discovery that run contrary to NASA's work is proof positive that we have entered an age in which objectivity in science is all but dead.

NASA has become a false god. While there is much to like about NASA, the organization engages in some very irresponsible practices. Since NASA has immersed itself in a game of selective apocalyptic scare tactics for the sole purpose of securing a never-ending stream of government handouts, let's look at their previously swept-under-the-carpet transgressions using the standards of science, Scripture, and laws of nature.

One of the concerns we should have about NASA is the amount of harmful pollution released by various rocket launches. Sources vary, but a typical space shuttle launch burns 2.2 million pounds of fuel to get into orbit.[65] When we add to this as many as one hundred smaller additional NASA launches in a typical year, and when we consider that this pollution is concentrated over a small geographical area, the potential harmful effects to fish, wildlife, water and air are indeed sizeable.

If you or I were to generate this type of negative environmental impact, we would surely be called out for it, and perhaps even fined or charged with a crime. NASA, however, a supposed protector of the environment is not called out for their poison. This is an important illustration of how those with perverted agendas are being allowed to direct mankind.

The NASA apologist will reject this idea and point out that our

---

65 https://coolcosmos.ipac.caltech.edu/ask/268-How-much-did-the-Space-Shuttle-weigh-.

automobiles, airports, and fossil fuel power plants generate many more times the pollutants than do rocket launches. Again, behold the hypocrisy! Can you imagine environmental activists allowing a major oil company the luxury of minimizing the effects of an oil spill by claiming that "compared to overall pollution problems, an oil spill is just a minor event?" They would never allow such marginalization. This favoritism is just another manifestation of scientific perversion.

If a pollutant is harmful to the environment, then regardless of where it comes from it needs to be publicized, reduced, and if possible, eventually eliminated. Giving NASA a free pass on irresponsible behavior simply because we revere their work, or because they support the godless ideology of the preferred political agenda short-changes mankind and the planet. It also perpetuates environmental abuse. We can't pick and choose what to speak out on based on how it plays against our own personal agenda. If we truly want to protect our environment, and our faith, then we must be equal and fair across the board.

Environmentalists, even liberal ones, may be shocked to learn that Scripture was demanding environmental responsibility long before it ever became a media talking point.

Numbers 35:33–34 ESV

You shall not pollute the land in which you live, for blood pollutes the land, and no atonement can be made for the land for the blood that is shed in it, except by the blood of the one who shed it. You shall not defile the land in which you live, in the midst of which I dwell, for I the Lord dwell in the midst of the people of Israel.

The takeaway here is that NASA is the worst kind of polluter. Because much of society has almost godlike and certainly cult-like worship of NASA, we have turned a blind eye to environmental transgressions for which other corporations and private entities are being raked over the coals. NASA must be held to the same standards as others.

Another concern we should have about the space program is that the rocket propellants used contain ozone-damaging constituents.[66] These chemicals are being released high in the atmosphere where their harmful effects are exponentially more intense than pollution that occurs on and near the earth's surface. Considering that more nations are entering space exploration, we can expect the harmful effects of rocket pollution to get worse. For the record, other items released into the atmosphere by NASA's rocket engines include carbon dioxide, aluminum oxide and soot, all contaminants that climatologists insist influence our environment. It is immoral and, in my mind, criminal to allow NASA to release harmful chemicals into the environment while government punishes fossil fuel companies and individuals for doing far less.

If it seems puzzling that so many would allow NASA to pollute while punishing others who do far less, one simply must recall the story of Barabbas to see how these people think.

Given the choice of freeing Jesus or the criminal Barabbas, the masses chose Barabbas to be freed. The reason they chose Barabbas is that Jesus spoke truth and morality. Jesus reminded people that they were sinners, that their immoral lifestyle was not acceptable. So, in their love of self they cut their own noses off to spite their face and sent our Lord to his death.

NASA you see is Barabbas to the perversionist for if scientific truth were to prevail, the belief in life on other planets, climate

---

66   https://www.cbc.ca/news/science/rocket-launches-environment-1.5995252.

change, diminishing resources and green technology would be forever exposed as lies. They would have to accept that the earth is indestructible, and that God's abundance is endless.

Let us look further into more evils of NASA.

Making matters worse for our environment, in addition to the chemical debris being released into the environment by NASA and other space programs, there is also a massive number of broken parts and jettisoned equipment from past space missions that remain trapped in orbit around the earth.[67] Also included in this debris is dust from solid rocket engines, paint flakes and chemical coolants. Some sources claim the number of junk particles to be in the millions. As more and more missions take place, especially with more nations entering space exploration, the technological junkyard that orbits our planet will continue to grow. This orbiting junkyard is so pronounced that new space vehicles must be fitted with protective shields to protect them in the likely event of collisions with this debris. Many particles of debris are large enough to cause devastating explosions in the event of direct collisions.

In 1978, NASA scientist Donald J. Kessler proposed a theory in which the high density of floating debris may reach a point where there are so many collisions just from the debris itself that future space exploration, GPS technology, and satellite use would be impossible. He projected a chain reaction that would create a vicious and randomly orbiting storm of dangerous debris. Navigating through this mess would be next to impossible. This theory is often presented as the *Kessler Syndrome*.[68] As NASA continues to dump junk into our orbit, and as other nations enter space exploration,

---

67   https://www.cbc.ca/news/science/rocket-launches-environment-1.5995252.
68   https://www.space.com/kessler-syndrome-space-debris.

the possibility of man destroying his own ability to explore space and launch satellites comes closer to being a reality.

People love looking at Hubble Telescope images, which of course are heavily and artificially doctored, colored, and filtered. However, if you would like to see truly amazing space photos, I suggest you search "pictures of space debris" on the Internet. I promise, when you witness the irresponsible, prolific deposit of junk that NASA has left blanketing our planet, you will think about space exploration in an entirely new light, and it won't be favorable.

It is crucial that we address this issue, because the massive amount of orbital junk reflects and refracts light in a multitude of ways, and as such, undoubtedly has a direct impact on the heating and cooling of the earth. Without hesitation, the potential negative effects of this orbital junkyard need to be investigated and a remedy found as soon as possible. There is a possibility that we have already deposited so much junk in our orbit that an actual Kessler Syndrome is inevitable. There is also the danger that a traveling meteor or asteroid could set off such a chain reaction of collisions among all the debris. NASA should be prohibited from further irresponsible behavior.

Leviticus 18:28 ESV

Lest the land vomit you out when you make it unclean, as it vomited out the nation that was before you.

I reiterate that we must accept that many of NASA's goals are knowingly or unknowingly focused on proving that God doesn't exist. To me, believing that there are other planets like earth, and that there is intelligent life on those planets is the ultimate attack on God.

In *Genesis 11:1–9* we are told the story of the Tower of Babel.

We recall that men set about building a tower to reach up into the heavens and set themselves apart from all others. We are told that because God saw that this effort was pompous and could only lead men away from him, he took action to confuse the workers by giving them all different languages. In so doing, God prevented men from communicating with each other and work on the tower ceased.

For some time now, I have believed the efforts of NASA to be eerily similar to those who went into building the Tower of Babel. The difference being that Babel sought to get close to God, while NASA climbs into the heavens so that it may denounce God and somehow disprove his existence. The net effort is the same; both endeavors fill man with self-importance and pomp. Both efforts draw man away from God.

I am not much for making predictions, but I am attentive and fearful of anything and anyone who mocks God. As more nations and private corporations have entered the space market the potential amount of damage to our planet and the amount of fanaticism about extraterrestrial life continues to grow by leaps and bounds. I cannot believe that God is pleased with NASA's mutilation of space. We should all fear the repercussions if he decides to stop this.

It is also wise for us to note that there is great instability in the modern space race. The different players do not always cooperate or share information with each other. The potential for catastrophes in space, and even wars over differences are becoming more likely every day. It is not hard to see that the space race has provided a new weapon for Satan to attack Christianity.

When you add to this astronomical Tower of Babel, the dangers presented by a potentially lethal orbiting junkyard, it becomes easy to see that the future of space exploration is not a bright one, and it is not in man's best interest.

When space exploration begins to self-destruct, and the signs are there to suggest it is already happening, it will be because NASA was pulled away from once being helpful to mankind and instead was turned toward attacking God's promises to us.

While unregulated pollution from space exploration continues uncontrolled, other irresponsible NASA behaviors also present challenges that demand our attention far more than fictional global warming. One of those dangers has to do with changing the overall level of matter and energy on earth.

Space exploration has removed millions of tons of fuel, precious minerals, and other materials from the earth, and has distributed them into space and even onto other planets. This certainly does not sit well with God. Let's take a scientific look at just how toxic sending earth's precious resources into space really is.

If we consider what Einstein taught us about mass and energy, we can see that space exploration has changed the mass and potential energy of the earth.

Einstein taught us that the total energy of any entity can be represented by the following equation.

$E = mc^2$

<u>Given:</u>

E = total energy
m = mass
c = the constant for the speed of light (186,000 miles per second)

Now, if we step back and realize that our space exploration has removed millions of pounds of material from the earth and redeposited it into orbit, on the moon, Mars, and other places, then we scientifically must conclude that NASA has reduced the total energy and mass of the planet.

Now, this does not mean NASA has found a way to destroy mass and energy, because they haven't. They have merely redistributed its location and sent much of it away from the earth. In this next equation let us look at the earth within the context of NASA's resource-depleting activities.

If we utilize the symbol λ to represent the total amount of energy NASA has removed from the earth and sent into space, the new Einsteinian equation for earth's reduced potential energy would appear as follows.

$$E = (m - \lambda) c^2$$

The NASA apologist will take two exceptions to my statements. Their first objection will be to argue that compared to the tremendous amount of total mass and energy of the earth, the total reduction in matter due to what has been sent into space is minuscule. Such a defense is frivolous and evasive of the facts. Let us examine why the amount of energy/mass NASA has removed from earth is indeed critical to mankind. This is an illustration of how our toolbox lesson about the relative relationships of numbers will serve us well.

NASA's potentially fatal behavior is illuminated in the c^2 part of this equation. The speed of light (c) is equal to a value of 186,000 miles per second, and when we square this number within the structure of Einstein's equation, we arrive at a multiplication factor of almost thirty-five trillion. Taken in full context, the "paltry" multiple tons of displaced matter that NASA wants us to believe are insignificant, when multiplied by a factor of almost thirty-five trillion, becomes alarmingly quite significant.

This exponential nature of energy equations explains why the seemingly small amount of mass that goes into a nuclear bomb can create such devastation when it is detonated. It also explains why just a small, seemingly insignificant amount of mass change in the wheel of a NASCAR vehicle, when subjected to high rates of revolution, can prove to be catastrophic.

The second and equally impotent objection the NASA apologist will make to my claims about depleting the earth of its mass and energy is to point out that a lot of mass constantly enters the earth from space. Their argument is that what we send into space is offset by what enters our atmosphere. Really? When was the last time a several-hundred-thousand-pound, rocket-sized rock landed on earth from space? I must have missed that event.

Most of what enters our atmosphere burns into small pieces. The matter that does land here is largely iron based[69] and cannot replace the precious elements that go into making equipment for space exploration.

Let's look at the physical manifestations this loss of the earth's energy potential can cause. Again, remember that while this exercise is theoretical, unlike climate change, the laws of science support my position.

In addition to changing the total potential energy of the earth, NASA's redistribution of mass has also changed the weight of the earth, and for that matter, the weight and potential energy of the

---

69   https://www.nationalgeographic.org/encyclopedia/meteorite/#:~:text=Stony%20meteorites%20are%20made%20up,some%20metal%E2%80%94nickel%20and%20iron.&text=Ordinary%20chondrites%20are%20the%20most,that%20have%20fallen%20to%20Earth.

moon, Mars, and any other entities where we have sent scientific equipment adding to their mass. To my knowledge, studies on these effects have not yet been explored to any great extent, but the laws of science tell us that this redistribution of mass does change the physical behavior of the planets involved.

Without exception, scientists agree that the gravitational force, orbit, and rotation of any object are intimately related to its mass.[70] Scientific logic tells us that a lighter earth will indeed begin to orbit closer to the sun. For those concerned about climate change, danger flags should be popping up all over the place.

If our orbit were to grow larger, earth's temperatures would continually increase as we pass closer to the sun and then dramatically increase at times we were furthest from the sun. Some of the expected changes would be that our oceans, lakes, and rivers would experience tremendous evaporation; our winds, rains and storms would grow more severe; our communications would be disturbed by growing electromagnetic and ionic interference; and our entire GPS technology would be threatened. Our protective ozone layer would be marginalized, and harmful solar radiation exposure on earth would increase. These are only a few examples of the theoretical cataclysmic effects that orbit change brought on by continued proliferation of NASA's mass depletion activities could bring upon our planet.

I want to be very careful to explain that this exercise does not contradict my position that man cannot alter God's planet, but instead demonstrates that those who claim to be saving the planet are the most egregious violators of good environmental stewardship.

Think about this. Climatologists struggle to make a credible

---

70   https://sciencing.com/relationship-gravity-mass-planets-stars-8487902.html.

correlation between carbon dioxide emissions and climate change, and as more evidence unfolds, this correlation appears to be less and less provable. However, if we consider their data, along with reported changes in our ice formations, oceans, and increasing health risks due to harmful solar radiation, we can credibly argue that the source of these changes is not CO2 emissions but instead the earth's physical changes brought on by NASA's redistribution of the earth's mass.

The lack of study in this area is a prime example of shallow conclusions being made about both climate and outer space. This is a prime example of perverted science.

This danger would be bad enough if all we had to worry about was the continuation of our clueless government encouraging the depositing of earth's precious resources all over space, but our planet now faces the additional threat from entrepreneurial buffoons who want to colonize Mars and send one-way spaceships bearing construction materials, food, water, technology, and a misguided group of lost souls to live there.

Unlike many of the ridiculous apocalyptic scenarios we have been shredding with science and Scripture, the eventual effects of changing the earth's natural behavior by transferring away mass and energy are described accurately by those same laws. Therefore, if we are really concerned about affecting our planet in a negative way, it is the transgressions of NASA that are worthy of our time, energy, and scrutiny. These are the type of relevant environmental topics we should be engaged in discussing.

We must remember that the precise stability of earth's orbit is responsible for the sustainability of all life. Our temperature, atmosphere and weather patterns are intimately connected to our orbit. The slightest change in this orbit threatens these life-supporting relationships. God, and the nature he gave us, is not going to let this happen, but we really don't want to live in a time when the earth decides to make a major self-adjustment to stop this behavior.

Redistribution of the earth's mass taken to extremes over time, would change the gravitational forces on the earth. While reduced gravitational force might be great for our jumping abilities, it would bring physical changes to every task and normal activity with which we engage. Vehicles would not have the traction, stability, or maneuverability they do now. Jets would have to be redesigned and pilots retrained to learn new landing and take-off reactions. Our bodies would function and develop differently, vegetation would grow taller, projectiles would travel further, matter would weigh less, and objects would fall at a slower rate. In short, if the earth's gravitational force were to change, we would have to rewrite every book of physics known to man. As silly as you might find this discussion, the relationship of mass to gravity is well documented throughout the history of science.

As a secondary but equally important consideration, we must also recognize that the transfer of matter doesn't just affect earth but also the places where we are adding mass. We need to ask what happens to the orbits and rotations of the moon and Mars as our activities contribute to their respective overall mass. A weightier Mars and moon will pull harder at their relative orbits in relation to the earth, the sun, and other planets.

As a side note, but a very important one, can you tell me by whose permission, by what consensus, and by what legal declaration NASA has the right to indiscriminately take from the earth and transfer into space any precious resource that they see fit? If one of us were to start removing flowers from the cemetery at Arlington to plant in some barren plot of land that we deemed in need of beautification we would be arrested. Yet NASA can rape and pillage any part of earth and scatter it about as litter wherever in the universe it sees fit. How can any man not find this irresponsible action to be a crime against science, mankind, and God?

Scripture also shows God to be insulted by NASA's ignorant, disrespectful behavior. Please, think again about the trash pile of precious resources they have scattered in orbit around our beautiful planet as you read the following Scripture.

Jeremiah 2:7 ESV

And I brought you into a plentiful land to enjoy its fruits and its good things. But when you came in, you defiled my land and made my heritage an abomination.

The saddest part in all of this is that NASA is trashing our planet because of a bitter, three-point, God-hating plan.

- To find life on other planets – life that does not exist!
- To find planets like earth – no such planets exist!
- To prove that God does not exist – *God created all things*!

Left un-policed, continued plans to transfer more and more resources from earth to other places will become more common. When so many here are in need, this behavior is irreprehensible.

For the record, if I haven't been clear, I am indeed calling for a halt to all space exploration. I do not believe that NASA or any other space exploration program has the right to transfer matter from earth to any other planet or entity. There has been a woeful lack of research and study on this topic, and as it stands now, man doesn't have even a vague idea about the ramifications of a mass transfer away from earth. If ever there was an area of study that demanded the collective effort of the world's scientists, it is this.

OK, I can hear my critics now! "Tommy, you go to great lengths to tell us God's earth is indestructible but then turn around and criticize NASA for depleting earth. Didn't you say that the earth is indestructible?"

Of course, the answer is that God's earth will never be destroyed, not by NASA, not by anything of this world. The earth will always right itself, heal itself and continue upon the path God intended for it.

However, it is the retaliation from God for man's disobedience that should strike fear into us. When God makes corrections for the actions of mankind, there is often great destruction, pain, and woe from his lessons. This is the danger NASA brings to humanity.

The point of this chapter was to show that NASA, by presenting only the information that suits its agenda, is a vicious weapon against Christianity and an offender of the very environment that it claims to be protecting. It demonstrates just how clever Satan has become at stealing souls and spreading pestilence. There has never been a more dangerous Trojan Horse than NASA.

Chapter Seven

Water, Precious Water

I have been intimately involved in the conservation, reclamation, purification, conditioning, altering, and manufacturing of water since I graduated college in 1981. Water remains one of the most misunderstood gifts of nature, and the folklore, mistruths, exaggerations, and perceptions of water boggle the imagination.

Climate change perversionists frequently talk about water scarcity, droughts, and a diminishing water supply as yet another way to suggest that God, the Creator, is incompetent and that only man and science can save the world's water supply. Here is a newsflash; there has never been, nor will there ever be, a shortage of water. There is no drought that can or will ever diminish civilization. There is the same amount of water on earth today as there was on the very day the planet was created.[71]

Water exists in a continuous cycle. It is consumed and taken up into the substance of man, animals, and plants; it is eliminated by man and animals; it evaporates, condenses and rains; it seeps into the ground; it feeds our lakes and rivers; and the entire process repeats itself continuously and infinitely. Nothing man can do will ever affect this cycle.

The phenomenon of water shortage doesn't exist. It is nothing

---

71   https://olc.worldbank.org/sites/default/files/sco/E7B1C4DE-C187-5EDB-3EF2-897802DEA3BF/Nasa/chapter1.html#:~:text=Earth's%20water%20is%20finite%2C%20meaning,does%20not%20increase%20or%20decrease.

more than a fabricated perception, a selfish one whereby man convinces himself that something is wrong with the earth unless it provides rain wherever and whenever needed. But the earth doesn't turn on man's schedule; it turns on its own. When men choose to build civilizations in areas with little available water to begin with, of course normal fluctuations in the planet's weather and precipitation cycles will loom much more critical. During normal, regular periods of drought, the perversionist loves to step up on a soapbox and create fear over how much the earth's water characteristics have changed. This is hogwash.

I happen to love the Las Vegas area and hope to persuade my wife to spend our golden years frolicking in the mountains and desert. Now, as much as I love that area, I realize that for man to flourish in the Mojave, new innovative water management techniques that include seawater, conservation, collection, and storage measures must be made. As we speak, water levels in Lake Meade are very low. Does this mean that something has changed in the earth's water cycle? No, it doesn't. All it means is that while the area has grown and added water users, man has not kept up with adequate infrastructure. Rest assured, the earth always provides rains to fulfill our water needs. Remove man from the Nevada, California, and Arizona areas and soon Lake Mead and the Colorado River will once again overflow in abundance.

The man who chooses to live by the ocean or Great Lakes will never in his life experience a shortage of water. Conversely, the man living in South Africa experiences water shortage not because of changes in climate or weather patterns, but because there are too many people competing for already limited available water. The problem with water shortage alarmists is the same as with climate alarmists—they have blinders on to any other causes or solutions that detract from their agendas.

As a side note, I am in no way minimizing the water difficulties of many South African villages, but those difficulties are man-made difficulties and have absolutely nothing to do with the earth, its climate, or its ability to quench the world's thirst. God provided water in abundance beyond our comprehension. Scripture reminds us of just how plentiful our bounty of water is.

Isaiah 44:3 ESV

For I will pour water on the thirsty land, and streams on the dry ground; I will pour my Spirit upon your offspring, and my blessing on your descendants.

Before moving forward, I want to again recall our discussion from chapter four about climate change and relate it to the supposed water shortage in California that has been used as a showcase for our impending climate apocalypse. During 2014 the Obama Administration released billions of gallons of fresh water out of California reservoirs, but not to farmers and citizens, but instead to rivers and streams in an effort to protect certain species of fish. The water released was enough to supply the needs of eighty million people.[72]

Later, when normal fluctuations in rainfall provided 50 percent less than an average year, the administration cried "climate change" and blamed God for their stupidity.

If you do not see this as a purposeful attack on God and our faith, if you do not see this as a clear example of Satan mobilizing perverted science and using it as a weapon against God's promise to us, a timeline recapitulation should add clarity to what is going on.

- Flush with water, California releases water to safe fish.

---

72   https://californiaglobe.com/articles/california-releasing-water-from-reservoirs-claiming-drought-conditions/.

- The water was enough to fill the needs of eighty million people.

- A completely normal fluctuation in rainfall fails to replenish what was released.

- California residents suffer water shortage and are forced to endure drastic conservation measures.

- Government blames the planet via climate change for the strife.

So that we understand the relentlessness of these kinds of attacks on us, let us stay in California just a bit longer for I tell you that these people, perversionists, loathe God to the point where they will accept self-destruction before bending their knee to him.

In 1973 Albert Hammond released the now famous hit song "It Never Rains in Southern California." If there ever was a more quintessential statement to document the foolishness and stupidity of man, I have never witnessed it.

Understand the gravity of this event. Almost fifty years ago, a hippie songwriter recognized that rainfall does not happen that often in Southern California. However, it took all that time for our top leaders, scientists, engineers, NASA, and government to realize the same thing.

Had Albert Hammond been elected governor of California back then there is a very good chance that the state would have been much better equipped to handle the always fluctuating precipitation patterns that they have historically experienced.

Sadly, this tongue-in-cheek reference does illuminate the sickening behavior of men who continually blame God for their own failures.

The Perversion of Science

It is an absolute misrepresentation and lie to suggest that California has been experiencing droughts of increased severity due to man-made climate change. The California-Nevada Climate Application Program (CNAP) demonstrates that since about 1990, the overall average rainfall in California has been above historical levels, and above normal.[73]

Statistics from WeatherNation TV show that since 1950, California has experienced greater rainfall than in many decades before.[74]

Is this true? Of course, it is, and as further evidence over the last decade it has become common practice for California to dump billions of gallons of fresh, clean water into local lakes and rivers due to the phenomenon that the abundant rain and snow God has been sending the state constantly overflows the available reservoir storage capacity.[75]

So, we see there is no such thing as climate change-induced drought in California. It is hogwash. It is blasphemy. What we do have is an ever-abundant blessing of water, a vigorously growing state, and failed, negligent leaders who never thought that instead of throwing away billions of gallons of water each year, it might be a good idea to build additional reservoirs/storage capacity to capture and harvest the bounty that God continues to send them.

In the face of great failure and water hardships these people blame God, the environment, and climate change. Let my message to you again ring clearly; any man who suggests that God and science are not in harmony, any man who dares suggest that the earth

---

73   https://cw3e.ucsd.edu/wp-content/uploads/2015/02/CA_Precip_final.pdf.
74   https://www.weathernationtv.com/news/rain-california-last-years-la-nina/.
75   https://insuremekevin.com/why-is-folsom-dam-releasing-so-much-water-flood-protection/.

is in peril and that man must change his behavior to save it is a perversionist of the worst kind. He is a blasphemer and an enemy of Christianity.

When speaking of the abundance of water on earth, the story of Noah surely comes to mind. The great flood is something pagans and those who pervert science love to criticize. They ask us, "If water covered the earth during the time of Noah, then why is only 75 percent of earth today covered in water? Where did all this flood water come from?"

This is a reasonable question and one that is surely hard for the Christian to answer. The challenge is even fortified by my own proclamation that there is the same amount of water on earth today as there was when it was created.

I can hear the perversionist say to himself, "We gotcha, Tom; surely the story of Noah could not have happened because there isn't enough water to cover all of the earth."

Once again, however, the news for the perversionist isn't good for you see there is in fact much more than enough water on earth for the land to have once been flooded completely and easily. Tom, are you crazy? Where is this water?

Before I deliver another smackdown to those who would blaspheme our God and his word, let us enjoy yet another refreshing assurance from God, and then behold his water magnificence.

Hebrews 11:3

By faith we understand that the universe was created by the world of God so that what is seen was not made out of things that are visible.

So here is the payoff. While these misguided fear mongers have been wasting trillions of dollars chasing non-existent aliens from other planets and looking for water in space, a group of actually credible scientists discovered that a mere four hundred miles under the earth's surface is enough water to fill our oceans three times over.

The water is found within a mysterious mineral called ringwoodite.[76] The water inside ringwoodite constantly moves in and out bringing water to the earth's mantle. The mantle: you know that important part of the planet that remains unseen and not visible?

Those who doubt God's promises will quickly complain that with current technology, harvesting this bounty of water is beyond our reach. However, it was not that long ago that we didn't have an answer for polio, or the ability to travel into space. It wasn't long ago people died from diseases that today are easily managed. Trust me, trust God, if man needed this water he would bless us with the scientific minds to go get that water.

God has placed an unimaginable amount of bounty in things that are as of now unseen to us. But make no mistake, as the needs of man change, just as with ringwoodite, God will make these things available and visible to us. He always has, hasn't he? Can you cite any time in history when man has not been making new discoveries pretty much daily? And still, an uncountable amount of Christmas gifts still lay unopened under our tree.

Can you imagine the new possibilities ringwoodite represents to drought-stressed areas of the world? Join me again in savoring the awesomeness of God, the Creator of all things.

Genesis 7:20 ESV

The waters prevailed above the mountains, covering them fifteen cubits

---

76   https://letstalkscience.ca/educational-resources/stem-in-context/ringwoodite-and-deep-water-cycle.

deep.

As Christians we must not only take delight and celebrate, but we must boast and proclaim to the world how millennium after millennium, century after century, decade after decade and year after year, without looking for it, God unveils new scientific discoveries and without fail leaves the perversionist, the detractors of our faith scratching their heads in defeat. I promise you, whatever the next potential apocalypse these vermin create, science and God will quickly dismiss it.

Not only do we now have proof that there is much more than an ample amount of water to have flooded the entire earth during Noah's time, but we can also dispel once and for all the equally idiotic theory that our water came to us from icy comets that once collided into the young, forming earth. The water was already here, under the earth's surface, just waiting to be released.

Gee, I wonder who put it there?

An interesting fact about the generous abundance of water supplied to earth is that depending on who you cite, only 1–2 percent of it is considered fit for human consumption and of that only 1–2 percent of it is available in bodies of water, with much of it being tied up in glaciers and ice formations.[77]

The good news is that this seemingly paltry amount is much more than mankind will ever require. Think about that for a moment. There are eight billion people on earth, and all our water needs are being met by less than 2 percent of the water God gave us. And we are running out of water you say?

---

77   https://dropinthebucket.org/water-facts/?gclid=Cj0KC-QiA_8OPBhDtARIsAKQu0gaaSoIjoNHUWvvQiCYil-aOoIIE_Ih-vG8km-tNYLhnRZo_5NoIuw3gaAu6XEALw_wcB.

Added to our overwhelming, abundant blessing of water, purification technology allows us to take aqueous solutions from hazardous industrial processes, sewage collection, lakes, streams, ponds, and anywhere else water accumulates, and turn even that into perfectly safe, EPA-approved drinking water. Even salt water, which represents 95 percent of the earth's water supply, is easily converted into safe drinking water.

Furthermore, all these sources, and even the dirtiest and radioactively contaminated water, can be purified far beyond the requirements for drinking water, up to USP water for injection, reagent grade laboratory water, and to the tougher-to-achieve E1 specification demanded by the electronics industry. In short, there is no water source on earth that cannot be made suitable for any aspect of human life.

This illuminates yet another blessing from God that we must recognize and celebrate as an inexhaustible abundance. It is the abundance of intelligent scientists who can harness the earth's provisions to facilitate the well-being of their fellow man.

Nature and technology constantly recycle the earth's abundant water. Water that you flushed today may very well be poured tomorrow into fine crystal glasses at one of New York City's finest restaurants. As an environmentalist and water treatment specialist, I have always chuckled to myself upon hearing an uppity restaurant patron bragging that he only drinks the finest water from the finest sources. Nature and God bring us all to the same watering trough!

Another area in which the perversionist misrepresents both the laws of God and science is in water purity. Is the world honestly running out of pure, clean water as these environmental alarmists would have us believe? To answer that, we need to acquire a better understanding of the nature of water purity.

As it turns out, pure water, by chemical definition is the molecule H_2O. An analytical examination of a sample of pure water would show no measurable contaminants and provide a resistance to electrical passage of roughly eighteen million ohms-cm, (18.2 megohms-cm to be exact).[78]

This resistance measurement is perhaps the most accepted benchmark for determining the purity of water. There is no industrial, medical/research, pharmaceutical, food, beverage, electronic or any other application that does not use resistance to electrical current as a fail-safe measurement in determining water purity from a mineral standpoint.

So where does one go to find pure water? Perhaps to the high mountains of Colorado where the ice-cold streams provide the cleanest water possible for great beer brewing, or perhaps to the frozen glaciers at our polar caps?

You may find it shocking to know that pure water does not exist in nature. It never did and never will. It is physically, chemically, and biologically impossible for pure water to exist in nature. Pure water is terribly unstable. When a raindrop is first formed it does, for the briefest fraction of a second, exist as pure water, but it doesn't remain pure long enough to take a measurement. The next part of our discussion explains why.

The H_2O molecule exists physically as a V-shaped structure with the oxygen atom at the base of the V and a hydrogen atom at each end of the V. For the sake of trivia, the angle between the V's arms is 104.5 degrees. The water molecule is called a dipole because it has a slightly positive electrical charge at the hydrogen end and a

---

[78] https://www.labmanager.com/white-papers-and-application-notes/resistivity-conductivity-measurement-of-purified-water-19691.

slightly negative charge at the oxygen end.[79]

You will recall from our toolbox that every system in nature that has energy strives to reach equilibrium by releasing that energy. In the same way that falling marbles eventually come to rest, the energized water molecule always seeks to relax its dipole electrical charges and come to rest. Because of the slight electrical charges, a water molecule has at its ends, it has potential energy that it would like to relieve. The water molecule relieves that energy by attaching itself to and dissolving anything it encounters. It is for this reason science calls the water molecule the universal solvent, and it is for this reason pure water cannot exist in nature.

If you take a cup of pure water and set it on a table, a short time later you would find that the pure water, simply by absorbing CO_2 from the available atmosphere, would come to equilibrium at an acidic pH of about 5.5. It wouldn't be the best-tasting water. If pure water were allowed to circulate through the copper pipes in your home, the water would attach itself to the positive charges in the copper metal. The result would be the dissolving of your pipes in a short amount of time.

The water that runs down our beautiful babbling brooks is not pure, and at no time in the history of the earth was it pure. Such water is filled with bacteria, organic slimes, molds, metals, biological waste, and anything else the water might encounter.

The resting state, that is, the happy state of the pure water molecule, is contamination. As a result, when the perversionist cries about our

---

[79] https://www.worldofmolecules.com/solvents/water.htm#:~:text=The%20dipolar%20nature%20of%20the%20water%20molecule&text=Since%20oxygen%20has%20a%20higher,difference%20is%20called%20a%20dipole.&text=Hydrogen%20bonding%20also%20gives%20water%20molecules%20an%20unusual%20behaviour%20when%20freezing.

degrading water quality, we need to remind him that it is natural for water to be contaminated.

As an illustration, the oceans consist of pure water that is essentially contaminated with salt. This contamination makes the ocean water very stable and predictable by keeping the electrical charges at the end of the water molecule occupied with opposite charges.

The drinking water in your community, even though it meets EPA standards and is perfectly fine to drink, is full of contaminants.

Many of the contaminants are not only harmless but may be beneficial as well. Contaminants like calcium, iron, and manganese all of which are contaminants found in many of the foods and vitamins we eat are good for us. Other contaminants such as lead, mercury, and aluminum while toxic in large concentrations, can be found in our tap water albeit in safe, almost non-detectable amounts.

The takeaway is that the water we drink, by nature, will always be contaminated in one way or another.

Yet another area in which the perversion of science is attacking faith and mankind is to shake our confidence in the water we drink.

The global water filtration market in 2018 was rated at $8.6 billion and anecdotal information has pegged it at over $13 billion today. I can promise you that a good portion of those sales was made possible by an apocalyptic purveyor injecting scare tactics into the global drinking water conversation.

You may wonder how the promotion of home water purification technology is applicable to perversionists attacking Christianity and science. Please, allow me to explain.

During my career, I have worked closely with architects, engineers, chemists, design firms, laboratory clinicians, chemical suppliers, EPA regulators, and other water purification professionals who design, build, certify and operate the nation's municipal water systems. I have always found this group of individuals to be among the most enlightened, moral, ethical, educated, concerned and diligent people on earth. I am glad to work with such people and am here to say that we all should be thankful that such caliber of men and women manage our precious water. I have never doubted that their gifts and the technologies of water purification are blessings from God. I have never doubted that when I turn on my faucet, safe, clean, clear water will fill my glass.

I believe that the scare tactics used to spread misinformation about water are an attack on God because they cause us to worry and mistrust those responsible for the delivery of water. While this attack is subtle, it is indeed yet another case of man insisting that our planet needs saving, and that we should not trust each other.

I do fully recognize that in recent times there have been many stories about drinking water contamination and water system failures. Since water purification relies heavily on human input of course, the delivery of our drinking water will never be perfect. However, the suggestion that something nefarious or apocalyptic is going on with our water and professionals can only be considered an attack on mankind.

Since the over-hyped crisis about our drinking water quality has created so many concerns, I thought I might take a small diversion and offer up a few pointers about how we can purify our drinking water.

Those with private wells have more exposure to contamination than traditional city water users since there is no treatment plant between the water supply and the faucet.

Where hardness, iron, and a sulfur smell (rotten egg smell) are an issue, the local water treatment service company can be a big help. The technologies used to remedy these problems are proven, age-old and safe. Well-users normally do well in seeking out such a service company.

When private wells are in proximity to geological exploration, fracking and mining, or when concerns over specific contaminants or land breaches occur, it does make sense to have a higher degree of awareness and a backup plan. The good news here is that most municipalities have professionals and services to help answer questions and determine actual contamination. God's abundant blessings include countless local water professionals. Don't go it alone. Help has been provided.

For most consumers, the risks associated with drinking municipal tap water are minimal. Municipalities employ chemists, biologists, lab directors, operators, and engineers who not only do a great job of preparing our water, but who are more than happy to help us out with our problems and questions. All it takes is an email or a phone call.

One of the more common complaints people have about their water is the chlorine taste or smell. This contaminant is added by water treatment companies to kill biological and viral organisms. We must remember that some of the worst plagues of mankind came about from drinking non-chlorinated water. Chlorine is a double-edged sword, because in certain concentrations it protects us while in higher concentrations it can be a health hazard. It can create precursor chemicals such as perchlorates that are believed to cause cancer.

In air and water, chlorine has a short chemical half-life. In other words, as soon as chlorine is added to water it begins to dissipate.

The challenge for the municipal water plant is that customers who live close to the point where chlorine is added will get one dose, but customers at the end of the distribution line will get a smaller dose.

To make sure that the customer at the end of the distribution line gets an adequate dose of chlorine, a larger dose than what is ultimately required is often injected at the water plant. As a result, the home closer to the water plant may notice a stronger chlorine odor or taste. As water travels down the pipe network to the more distant customer, the chlorine will dissipate and be much less pronounced. The half-life of certain chemicals is one of the reasons two different customers of the same water provider can have tap water that tastes very different.

However, as with so many other protective, self-regulating provisions God has made for us, he has done so with this miracle sanitizing agent. Chlorine does its job and kills organisms and then for consumers who don't like chlorine, leaving a pitcher of water in the refrigerator for a few hours will allow the chlorine to decline in concentration, ultimately until there is none left.

However, if you want an even faster way to get rid of chlorine and odors in your water, God has provided yet another natural way for us to drink safe water in the form of granular activated carbon filters (GAC).

GAC filters are available in many types of disposable, user-friendly formats. Refrigerator GAC-based water filters are impregnated with silver particles to offer protection against bacteria. In addition, the low temperature of our refrigerators greatly reduces the ability of bacteria to grow. These filters make good sense on any type of tap water feed.

The interesting thing about GAC is that it is made from charring (pyrolyzing) otherwise discarded plant material such as clam shells and coconut shells.

The beautiful point to be gleaned here is that for many people experiencing water problems or wanting a higher level of water security, God has packaged a bundle of benefits including natural chemistry and man-made filters that can even be manufactured from otherwise useless plant byproducts. God invented green, and we don't have to lift a finger to be immersed in it.

For more complicated water concerns, there are more elaborate home treatment systems that include reverse osmosis, ultraviolet and even ozone technology. Systems can be large enough to provide purification for an entire house or small enough to handle normal drinking water demands. There are even simple-to-use DIY test kits that enable us to test our own water.

In addition to these water tools, we are blessed to have an abundance of companies that provide safe, delicious bottled drinking water. Whether we need water when we are traveling, enjoying outdoor activities, or even suffering through natural disasters, water is always available to us.

To close this chapter, I want to clarify that there are both good and bad applications of water products. There are many sensible situations in which we need help with contaminated, or scarce water. In those cases, the Lord has provided an abundance of technology and people who can help us.

However, when the sale of these products relies on the promotion of government agenda and scare tactics based in fear of water apocalypses, then water safety has been used as a weapon against God's promises to us, and it looms as yet another illustration of the

The Perversion of Science

perversion of science.

Chapter Eight

Oil, Precious Oil

No technological phenomenon has had more impact on humans than the discovery of crude oil. From the uncovering of the very first oil well to the creation of the world's most modern refineries, oil has always been and remains king of man's energy needs. Next to animals, plants, water and air, oil is the most important natural resource available to us. There will be no major shift in reducing man's dependence on crude oil for many generations to come.

There may be a forced action to use less oil by governments, but that does not change the reality that the oil God has given us remains the single cleanest, most natural, most efficient way to convert energy for our blessed lifestyle.

Carbon chemistry, also known as organic chemistry, allows men to manipulate chains of carbon atoms to create the vital necessities of our modern lives.

We depend on oil to fire the engines of cars, planes, construction/demolition equipment, mining vehicles, ships and trucks carrying goods. The distillation of oil provides many derivatives used in medicine, food and beverage products, cosmetics, soaps, paints, varnishes, pesticides, biocides, solvents, plastics, tires, tar, water treatment products and chemicals, computers, electronics, forestry equipment and even the artificial kidneys that maintain the lives of patients stricken with renal failure.

Without crude oil there can be no electric cars, solar panels, hydroelectric plants, wind technology or any other nonsensical, so-called clean energy.

There is an immense multitude of life-giving products that require oil for their manufacturing process. There is not a man, woman, or child on earth whose life is not enriched by the science and blessing of oil. Without it, the modern way we live would cease to exist, and countless pleasures, comforts, safeties, and conveniences that we take for granted would no longer be possible.

Fortunately, we don't have to worry. Scripture assures us that God has provided more oil than we will ever need or want. I never tire of quoting the following Scripture and take great joy in again sharing the power of God's promise.

Matthew 6:26 NIV

Look at the birds of the air, they do not sow or reap or stow away in barns and yet your heavenly Father feeds them. Are you not much more valuable than they?

I assure you, God's promise of abundance also applies to oil, just as it applies to water, food, heroic policemen and firemen, and even the brilliant minds, many yet unborn, who will solve tomorrow's problems and bring us newer and more fascinating technologies and discoveries.

Perceptions about oil vary widely. While some fret they may someday be unable to get their fair share, others condemn its consumption. Many want to conserve oil, and still others want America to free itself from its dependence on it.

One thing is certain; the subject and science of oil remain a hotly debated, widely misunderstood topic that often finds opponents red-faced and sporting clenched fists. It is hard enough to find two people with the same views on oil, let alone find a consensus within the general population on how we should use it.

Am I saying that man will never run out of oil? No, not at all. What I am saying is that it does not matter if we run out of oil. It has no future significance for our existence. It is vital and necessary in the here and now. God put it here for us to use. He commands us to work hard, prosper, and not be afraid of running out of things.

God never promised us anything but abundance. So, a Christian who really understands this promise knows that as our oil reserves begin to dwindle, his blessing of abundance will take care of us. New scientists, new discoveries, new fuels, and technology we have not yet imagined are all part of God's plan for us. Oil is here for us to use. There is no other debate needed.

Isaiah 41:13

For I, the Lord your God, hold your right hand; it is I who say to you, "Fear not, I am the one who helps you."

You may ask what the consumption and management of oil have to do with God or with the perversion of science. As we proceed, you may be surprised to learn that the topic of oil is yet another battleground where non-believers and perversionists attack Christianity and God.

The first and most vicious oil-related attack on Christianity is orchestrated by those who predict doom and gloom if our oil supply is depleted. The following highlights four illuminate why the worry about oil is damaging to mankind and to people of faith.

1. *The worry over oil implies that God didn't supply enough of something we need.*

Never has man been left without any vital resource. We have

always enjoyed an abundance of earth's precious resources, and no resource shortage ever predicted by a scientist has ever come to fruition. Even the most negative prognosticators admit that the earth still offers us many years of crude oil supply.

Because most of the earth is not only uninhabitable but unexplored, there is an unimagined bounty of yet-to-be-discovered oil gifted to us from God. Isn't it amazing that every few years someone "accidentally" stumbles upon a wealth of previously undiscovered fossil fuels? These facts cause the perversionist to choke on his own fear-mongering.

The lessons of abundance and fearlessness are clear. God advises us to work hard, to be without worry, to use the resources given to us and let him worry about tomorrow. Make no mistake, anyone who expresses fear about running out of fossil fuels is attacking Christianity.

In response to those who rebuff my faith, I in turn snub their perverted bastardization of science and remind them that despite their voluminous amount of past apocalyptic predictions of massive floods, earthquakes, volcanoes, ice ages, super-storms, Y2K havoc and other impending world doom, faith in the Creator has without exception, trumped their Chicken-Little foolishness, and will continue to do so. Man will never have an oil crisis other than what he creates artificially for personal gain.

2. *The worry over oil implies that the earth can never again produce oil.*

The satanic, godless attack that is this unfounded concern over oil supply comes from the fact that our government is promoting worry among the public, wasting money on foolish alternative technologies, and in general ignoring people who desperately need economic, medical, and vocational help.

I assure you that not only is earth indeed capable of once again producing oil but it is doing so as we speak. The cycle of life on our planet constantly returns organic matter to the soil, and the forces of nature that existed when our fossil fuels were created are still intact today. As we speak, the earth is converting organic matter into new fossil fuel. Am I saying that the earth will replenish oil faster than it can be used at our current rate of consumption? Of course not. It took many years for our oil supply to be produced, and if God allows our planet to thrive for generations to come, earth will continue to create oil. Our future may very well thrive from new yet undiscovered wonders, but it is scientifically incorrect to say the earth will never again create crude oil.

Perversionists gauge earth's performance in man's time, but the earth turns in God's time. Man creates his own conditions of civilization and then idiotically deduces that if the earth does not behave in a way that supports those choices, it means that somehow the earth is failing. That we chose to adapt our civilization to fossil fuels is our issue. Make no mistake, allowed the same time to work its magic, earth will again manufacture fossil fuels.

3. *The worry over oil ignores that God will provide new scientists and new technology to reduce our need for oil.*

As I have pointed out, we must remember that necessity has always been the mother of invention, and as with all technology, as the cost and difficulty of oil drilling increase, there will be a corresponding economic pressure for man to come up with alternatives. Throughout the history of mankind, new inventions and technologies have always been developed by someone who recognized a vital need and then used his God-given talents to fulfill it.

The automobile replaced the horse and buggy, anesthesia replaced taking a big gulp of bourbon, and so too will the future bring us new convenience and service. Right now, man doesn't have a need, other than a politically driven one to reduce the dependence on oil. It is abundant in supply, and it is inexpensive.

To see the real-world validation of what I say one can simply behold the host of new, agenda-driven, impotent energy alternatives being used to promote the idea that God's earth is impotent.

As we read about solar panels, roller skate-sized electric cars and pinwheels mounted high atop steel towers more and more we read accompanying stories of their failures, inadequacies and how they are falling short of curbing our dependence on oil. While all these technologies are already in motion, none of them scratch the surface of replacing oil. Even the perverted pundits of these things admit that they are so expensive, inefficient, and cumbersome that they cannot flourish without government subsidies.[80]

Many of our leaders lack faith, and as such, are motivated by fear, disinformation, and confusion. With these shortcomings is it any wonder that they are leading our country to abandon God's abundance, and potentially destroy our economy and our way of life?

Elon Musk, the largest builder and promoter of electric cars, has stated that there is not enough production of electricity to power these cars should they gain mass acceptance. To do so would require immense increases in our electricity production, new power lines, charging stations, and infrastructure; all things that require mining, minerals, and increased consumption of oil.[81]

80 https://www.christenseninstitute.org/blog/going-global-with-green-energy/?gclid=Cj0KCQiAosmPBhCPARIsAHOen-NiygYsTppiQOY-RH-x8fs0EsraSg9wr4IYFUSCdvNEdUcKN9AUv-l8aAqLtEALw_wcB.
81 https://www.barrons.com/articles/tesla-elon-musk-elec-

I am here to tell you that the ironclad evidence that these new "clean" technologies are driven by the evil purpose of attacking Creation is that they have to be forced, manipulated, and funded by government. When technologies are wholesome, and when they come from the Creator, they flow freely and are readily accepted by man.

Think about the introduction and immediate acceptance of inventions like motor vehicles, television, commercial flight, radio, penicillin, Kool-Aid, The Twist, Hula-Hoop and polyester. These inventions were so magnificent, so blessed that no force-feeding to the public was necessary.

One day in the future, oil will indeed become harder to harvest and more expensive to obtain. When that happens, it will not be by government handouts and impotent inventions that man changes the way he travels, manufactures, and discovers; it will be by technology and brilliant individuals that will be brought to us by the very highest source of scientific discovery—they will be brought by God.

Whatever the next great oil-replacement technology is, I guarantee you it will not be the invention of a politician, entertainer, or activist.

4. *The worry over oil promotes fear, confusion, and panic. It causes man to foolishly waste precious resources on imagined apocalyptic scenarios instead of spending those precious resources on people and tasks that truly make a difference.*

As the perversionist looks at man's existence, his understanding is that of a child. He can only view future society in terms of today's society. That being the case, he frantically fears running out of oil, and he frantically works to force the increased use of tric-vehicle-production-51633202912.

impotent technologies. The perversionist is misguided to the point of believing that he is helping to create earth-saving miracles.

On the other hand, in keeping with the recurring theme of this book, we know that a wise man, a Christian, is confident knowing that God has never, nor will ever, let mankind falter for lack of natural resources.

This difference in the perceptions of our existence will never be resolved as we believers have ease and comfort about our future. We accept that worldly things will change and take comfort in knowing that God will provide us with what we need to live amid these changes. Conversely, the pagan clings to life as he knows it today and is terrified that his worldly existence faces change. The perversionist will continue to be cursed by meaningless, frantic worry, and driven by evil, and we must not allow this to shake our trust in God.

Malachi 3:10 ESV

Bring the full tithe into the storehouse, that there may be food in my house. And thereby put me to the test, says the Lord of hosts, if I will not open the windows of heaven for you and pour down for you a blessing until there is no more need.

Proverbs 3:10

Then your barns will be filled with plenty, and your vats will be bursting with wine.

Isaiah 55:1 ESV

Come, everyone who thirsts, come to the waters; and he who has no money, come, buy and eat! Come, buy wine and milk without money and without price.

<u>Genesis 27:28</u>

May God give you of the dew of heaven and of the fatness of the earth and plenty of grain and wine.

Lest anyone suggest that I am zealously overstating how evil and scientific perversion comes into play in the discussion of oil and alternative energy sources, let me remind them that over the past several decades there has been no issue that has brought more war, terrorism, and loss of life than the conflicts surrounding oil production. There is no issue that has caused more government conflict or attracted more wealth.

Be clear! The consumption of oil is scientifically natural and is of God. The restriction and condemnation of it is a perversion that at its roots is driven by evil.

To close this chapter, I want to dispel the ridiculous notion that the consumption of oil is problematically polluting to earth. Imagine the stupidity of this as it suggests God gave us a resource that he knew would destroy us.

As we covered in our toolbox, there is no such thing as a clean energy conversion process but let us take a short scientific deviation to fortify my statements.

In science and engineering there are two important universal conventions called mass balance (MB) and energy balance (EB).[82] It is these scientific processes, and not political agenda or university studies that determine which processes are the cleanest and most efficient.

MB and EB allow the scientist to examine all the benefits a process may provide, and then document and record all the pollution, <u>hidden costs,</u> and other impacts associated with that process.

82   https://beeindia.gov.in/sites/default/files/1Ch4.pdf.

It is only by these processes that man can accurately compare technologies to each other.

Oil is a carbon-based material. Its consumption absolutely produces waste materials that include methane, carbon dioxide and water. So, do those things automatically mean that oil is a bad technology? Let us look closer.

Humans, just like combustion engines, also use carbon-based compounds to "make" energy. Like combustion engines, the human body creates waste that includes carbon dioxide, methane, and water (perspiration and urine). Neither engines nor the human body can function without consuming hydrocarbons and producing waste.

However, because machines are built of materials much stronger than human bodies, they are more efficient when it comes to units of energy produced per waste unit produced.

For instance, if we asked a group of men to manually pick up and transport an illegally parked car a mile, we would likely find it would require the hiring of thirty men each lifting 125 pounds to accomplish the task. It would likely take them a few hours to complete the task and along the way they would need food to supply the energy, and of course associated trips to the bathroom to eliminate waste.

Conversely, if we hired a tow truck, it would require perhaps a quarter gallon of gasoline and twenty minutes of work.

Clearly, the truck would require less energy, less time, less cost, and it would produce less waste than thirty men at work. The MB/EB analysis would favor choosing the tow truck over the hiring of thirty workers.

In the very same manner, when we do an MB/EB of oil-based technology compared to so-called clean technologies, the oil-based technologies always come out the clear winner.

Unseen in the clean technologies is their great destruction of land and water required to mine the required minerals required in production. Also unseen is the great amounts of oil and pollution involved with the mining and transport equipment, and high number of generating plants that must be built to equal the power output of just one conventional fossil fuel process.

MB/EB analyses are infallible. They tell the truth, and they are born of the science God gave to us. Therefore, it is no surprise that the perversionist hides such analyses in the lies that they advocate.

Always remember that I advocate responsible environmentalism. I have never advocated something that will hurt our planet. What I profess is contrary to the typical environmentalist, but let us be honest, most of what is good, wholesome, and godly is offensive to these people. With that said, I have no interest in peacefully coexisting or finding a middle ground with those who pervert science and blaspheme God. Scientific truth supports God and will always anger these people.

I advocate for taking care of what God has blessed us with. Indeed, we Christians should not consume in gluttony, but we should also not stop consuming because of fear. It is by faithfully using God's abundance, including oil, that we can prosper and be a blessing to others.

The following Scripture provides a clear message, Whether it is gold or oil we must be bold and fearless in using his gifts to us. Those who advocate not using oil for fear of destroying earth are perversionists, and they attack our Lord.

The Perversion of Science

Matthew 25:14–30

For it will be like a man going on a journey, who called his servants and entrusted to them his property. To one he gave five talents, to another two, to another one, to each according to his ability. Then he went away. He who had received the five talents went at once and traded with them, and he made five talents more. So also, he who had the two talents made two talents more. But he who had received the one talent went and dug in the ground and hid his master's money.

So, take the bag of gold from him and give it to the one who has ten bags. For whoever has will be given more, and they will have an abundance. Whoever does not have, even what they have will be taken from them. And throw that worthless servant outside, into the darkness, where there will be weeping and gnashing of teeth.

And here, additionally, we are instructed to build, invent, and prosper.

Exodus 35:10 ESV

Let every skillful craftsman among you come and make all that the Lord has commanded.

As I finish this chapter, I feel the same anxiety to illuminate how Satan has cleverly bastardized oil science and technology to destroy Christianity. I don't think I can ever stress enough just how he has disguised as seemingly harmless, even uplifting stories of science his newest weapons against our faith. Such is my journey.

Chapter Nine

Little Green Men

By far, for me, the worst attack on God is the ridiculous notion that there is intelligent life on other planets. NASA has used this perversion for years to capture the nation's attention and milk the government for billions of dollars. In so doing NASA has made a great effort to assure itself of a self-perpetuating arrangement. America has a love affair with ET and NASA is an expert at exploiting it.

Be confident; there is no life on other planets. There are no UFOs. There are no little green men. There are no planets that can sustain life. Man is the unchallenged top of the food chain in all of God's Creation. We are the only intelligent life in the universe, our animals are the only animals in the universe, and we, man, have domain and responsibility over all of it.

Genesis 1:26

Then God said, "Let us make man in our image, after our likeness. And let them have dominions over the fish of the sea and over the birds of the heavens and over the livestock and over all the earth and over every creeping thing that creeps on earth."

Neither the Mayans nor anyone else on earth was ever visited by beings from another planet. Crop circles and UFOs captured on video don't come from outer space, but instead come from nincompoops with too much time on their hands. The entire pursuit of life on other planets is not just buffoonery, it is a purposeful attack on God.

As it turns out, both Scripture and science proved long ago that the only intelligent life in the universe is on earth. Why non-believers are so offended by being uniquely blessed by the Creator, I have no idea, but whether they like it or not, man is the pinnacle of all that God has created.

I will disprove the buffoonery of life on other planets in the same irrefutable, orderly manner that I've used in the prior chapters. We will examine Scripture and then fortify those Scriptures with the laws of science. The non-believer will moan as I begin this discussion with another quote from Genesis. In the beginning …

<u>Genesis 1:27 ESV</u>

So God created man in his own image, in the image of God he created him; male and female he created them.

This is a pretty ironclad proclamation for the uniqueness of man. Long before discussions of aliens, the Bible gave witness that man was created to look like the Creator. In fact, the Son of God was created in the same image.

It is moronic to think that God would create man in his image and then say to himself, "I will now create a better, more superior being for another planet, and I will create this being in the image of someone else."

Rest assured, God, like any worldly father, saves the best for those he loves the most. Worldly fathers revel in seeing their offspring or adopted children walk, talk, speak, behave, and live a similar life to their own. God takes the same enjoyment in us.

In creating us in his image God left absolutely no room for a being superior to man.

While the following Scripture is not often thought of in terms of life on other planets, it speaks to me as a telling guarantee that there is indeed no such thing.

2 Peter 3:10 ESV

But the day of the Lord will come like a thief; the heavens will disappear with a roar; the elements will be destroyed by fire, and the earth and everything in it will be laid bare.

Scripture is telling us that not only will man not know when the last day is coming, but that on that day God will bring an end to the earth and man, and also to the universe.

It simply isn't logical to think that God would have created intelligent life elsewhere and then left their fate in the hands of man. Surely, if the Father created other intelligent beings, he would have loved them as well and would not have condemned them at our hands. He would have provided for them as he did for us, giving them free will, choice and salvation. But God only mentions these blessings as they apply to man, and for good reason.

By far, the most compelling proof that there is no intelligent life in the universe other than man can be found in perhaps the most beautiful and telling Scripture of all.

John 3:16 ESV

For God so loved the world, that he gave his only Son, that whoever believes in him should not perish but have eternal life.

God gave his only son to die for us. Clearly, this man, Jesus, could only have walked, taught, lived, suffered, and died once, on one planet. His blood could have only been shed to save one people.

Again, as Genesis tells us, in the beginning God created man. This was his last step before standing back and watching our civilization unfold. He created no other intelligent life forms after us or before us.

Let us now look at how science also proves that there is no life on other planets, nor has there ever been.

The perversionist maintains that the earth has been around for billions of years. For the sake of debunking this extraterrestrial bull schnitzel we will accept that supposition.

Let us also agree that for as long as the earth has been in existence, it has been bombarded by foreign objects, meteors, asteroids, gasses, radiation and who knows what else from origins all across the universe. Reportedly, many of our craters, valleys, canyons and even lakes and rivers were formed by huge particles from space ripping through our atmosphere and crashing into the surface of the planet. And let's not forget that all the other celestial bodies we have been probing and poking with our spacecraft and fancy telescopes have also been likewise bombarded with foreign objects since the beginning of time.

It should amaze us then that over billions of years with constant collisions from outer space, in numbers far too vast for us to comprehend, none of the specimens studied have ever been found to show traces of life.

- We have found no animals, fossils, bacteria, viruses, spores, yeasts, molds, or fungi in space.
- We have found no DNA or RNA.
- We have found no polypeptides, proteins, amino acids, or even simple organic chemicals indicative of living organisms.

Remember, not only do we have supposed billions and billions of years and collisions worth of samples from earth, but we also have voluminous samples taken from places like the moon and Mars that also render a big bunch of nothing.

What about UFO sightings? With all the Hubble Telescope searching, in all the countless light years of pictures that have been taken, have we come across any spacecraft? What about signs of civilization on all these telescopic images? Ancient ruins? Roads? Cities? Amusement parks? Again, the answer to all of this is a resounding no.

Our demolition of this ET stupidity gets even worse as we apply common sense. Forensics tell us that humans always leave evidence behind. Let's face it, we are a messy lot. We junk everything up.

Heck, we were hardly on the moon long enough to watch an episode of *Star Trek* and we left a ton of garbage behind. Anyone visiting the moon afterward would surely know that man was up there, because it looks like someone had a frat party.

Among other things we left was a titanium plaque announcing that man visited and came in peace. We left ninety-six bags of urine and feces, twelve pairs of space boots, artwork by Andy Warhol and others, a falcon's feather, two golf balls, a picture of one astronaut's family, and an obituary plaque of astronauts who died.[83]

God only knows what other stuff we left up there.

Putting Scripture and science aside for a moment, the concept of extraterrestrials even defies common sense. Every living thing leaves traces of it its life, work, and habits.

<u>Animals leave</u> tracks in the snow, husbands leave cookie crumbs

---

83   https://www.vox.com/2015/3/8/8163259/moon-objects-weird.

on the couch, park visitors leave trash in bins, moviegoers leave popcorn on the floor, criminals leave DNA, and look at what Frank Sinatra, Dean Martin, Van Gogh, and Beethoven left behind for us.

Yet the little green men? They don't urinate, defecate, leave footprints or trash? They don't leave recordings, radio messages, debris, or their own plaques to announce that they were there? And these are intelligent beings? They are smarter, more peaceful and loving than us?

WWII soldiers left the message "Kilroy was here" all over Europe to let other GIs know they weren't alone.[84]

Ancient people left writings inside caves and on mountain rocks to communicate with others who might pass by. Wives leave little notes with lipstick kisses to let husbands know they are being thought of. We leave tips on the counter to let hotel cleaning help that they are appreciated. And to repeat, we left a plaque to tell others who came to the moon that earthlings were there, and we came in peace.[85]

We leave evidence because we are living beings, and we leave other evidence because we are civil, kind, and compassionate for the well-being of others.

To imagine an intelligent being who would travel near us and not leave evidence to bond with us is to be an imbecile hell-bent on creating chaos, misinformation, and blasphemy. Even the simplest, ancient man reached out to the rest of Creation.

The reason man cannot produce evidence of Bigfoot, the Loch

---

84   https://www.thoughtco.com/killroy-was-here-4152093.
85   https://starchild.gsfc.nasa.gov/docs/StarChild/space_level2/apollo11_plaque.html.

Ness Monster or poltergeists is because these things are food for nincompoops. They do not exist. The same holds true for extraterrestrials and UFOs. They do not exist. If these things existed there would be evidence; there would be leftover debris.

I want both Christian and the perversionist to understand that the net result of billions of dollars spent on space exploration, the Hubble Telescope, NASA, and septillions of intergalactic depositions of debris onto our world, coupled with countless millions of lab samples, is that we don't have one stinking sign of evidence that there is life anywhere but on earth.

In the meantime, tens of millions go without health care, food, and safe water. Do you still doubt that Satan dances in delight at the vision of what space exploration is doing to mankind?

How hypocritical is it that the climate perversionist demands that we accept his climate change buffoonery based on only one hundred years of widely varying, non-standardized observations, yet when we bring up intergalactic collision samples from trillions of years that show no signs of anything, the same perversionist claims that our sample size is not large enough?

Make no mistake, the sample size for finding extraterrestrial life is indeed large enough for us to make a definitive conclusion. There is nothing out there.

In addition, if there is life on other planets, then why don't any of them have a space junkyard floating around their orbit like earth? Why aren't there signs of such orbital waste anywhere else? And once again, we are to believe that it is Christians whose faith and beliefs are unfounded in science? No kidding?

As I stated earlier, Americans are in love with the idea of life on other planets and from the earliest days of science-fiction audiences this genre of entertainment has continued to grow in popularity. From *Star Trek* conventions to *Area 51* annual migrations, to movies like *Aliens, Superman* and *Prometheus,* millions of enthusiasts wait around the corner for the next new fantasy. Pop culture is so engulfed by science fiction that even many science professors and cosmologists don't realize that they have blurred the boundary between science and fiction and in so doing have completely lost sight of reality.

People who believe in this extraterrestrial nonsense readily and proudly insist that the goober from outer space is superior to man. He is more intelligent and peace-loving. He watches over the universe with a knowing, paternal hand. Frequently when asked, "Why do these beings not contact us?" the answer given is because we are not yet smart enough to accept them.

That is like saying your Father is going to let you accidentally cut your finger off because you are not smart enough yet for him to teach you how to use the saw.

There are no beings smarter than man. Faults aside, man has cured diseases, mastered flight, harnessed electricity, given to the less fortunate, created beautiful art and music, built schools, and invented technologies that make life easier and more enjoyable. Our accomplishments are a testament to our Creation. Sadly, our weaknesses remain to hold us back, but those are our choices, not God's.

Where did this concept of superior intelligence in space come from? It came from television.

In the 1951 movie *The Day the Earth Stood Still*, an alien lands on earth and tells the people that they must live peacefully or be destroyed as a danger to other planets.[86] In the 2008 remake, the

---

86   https://www.imdb.com/title/tt0043456/.

alien Klaatu played by Keanu Reeves informs mankind that the earth is not "their" planet but instead is property of the intergalactic community. Klaatu proclaims that before it destroys the universe,[87] mankind must be eliminated so the earth can be restarted from scratch.

In the movie *Prometheus,* earth travelers believe that space giants are the Creators of man. In Star Trek, many episodes feature powerful, all-knowing races that recognized man as inferior, destructive, and primitive.[88]

Consider now that many of the charlatans and perversionists who regurgitate this idiocy are professors who teach it as science. Even prominent elected officials facilitate the wasting of billions of tax dollars on this buffoonery. For those of you who think that my concerns over the study of aliens being an attack on God are over the top, keep reading.

NASA gave a $7 million grant to Sarah Johnson, a Georgetown University biology professor, to develop a new detection system for discovering life on Mars. The professor calls her research project the *Laboratory for Agnostic Biosignatures.*[89]

Now I must ask you, if this woman and her study are purely scientific, why does she need to mention agnosticism in her study? What scientific purpose is served by her bringing a view of God into her work?

The answer is very simple. Those who believe in life on other planets only do so because of their hate for God. Anyone driven by science readily abandons this belief. It is only the pagan, the

---

87 https://www.imdb.com/title/tt0970416/.
88 https://www.imdb.com/title/tt1446714/.
89 https://starchild.gsfc.nasa.gov/docs/StarChild/space_level2/apollo11_plaque.html.

disciple of Satan, knowingly or not, who seeks to find life outside the boundaries of earth.

Continuing, the most popular justification the perversionist uses to defend his belief in extraterrestrial life is the statement that "The universe is so vast, the planets so large in number, surely there must be life out there."

I have a newsflash for you: there is no scientific correlation between the size or number of a sample and the possibility of a phenomenon existing.

As an example of this fraudulent thinking consider that our oceans are vast, almost beyond our imagination. If you were to assume that because the oceans are so vast, surely if you were able to fish long enough in the oceans you would eventually catch a largemouth bass. But you see, no matter how vast the ocean, no matter how long you fished, no matter how many different locations you explored, the possibility of catching a largemouth bass in the ocean is still zero.

The bass is a freshwater fish, and it only exists in fresh water. Fish for a billion years and you will never catch a largemouth bass in the ocean.

As much sense as this example makes, every mathematical model that predicts the possibility of life on other planets uses the same imbecilic logic that if something is large enough, repetitive searches will deliver the desired result.

In the absence of a single scientific piece of evidence proving life exists on another planet, the mathematician has created models so complex that the average person, unable to decipher the work, concludes that indeed life must exist in space.

Scripture, common sense, and science agree, there is no higher life form than man. There is no life anywhere but where God placed it—earth!

Chapter Ten

Indestructible Earth

In the fall of 1973, I had the good fortune to undertake Biology 501 under the guidance of a professor I only remember as Dr. Kreutzer. In addition to classroom and laboratory study, I spent many hours conversing with him about the *bios*, his specialty and life's passion. The bios I learned is a Greek word meaning "life." In my day, before the computer anagram BIOS, bios referred to the study of all living things and how they depend on and impact each other.

The most forceful and significant thing I learned from Dr. Kreutzer was that earth and man are indestructible. I also learned that man cannot affect anything about this relationship.

How uncanny was this that unbeknownst to me the things I was learning back then would one day become weapons for me to debunk the apocalyptic perversions that I am now addressing?

Even more astonishing is that as time went forward, the very concepts I was learning in science classes would later in life be reinforced by the Bible. To this very day, I get goosebumps when I talk about these experiences.

Accordingly, I believe this chapter is the most important part of the book. If people come to understand just how indestructible the earth is, and just how insignificant our impact is on it, then the perversionist will no longer be able to create worry, strife, doubt, and otherwise use science as a weapon against God.

Later in the chapter I cite some popular Scripture in which the earth is spoken of as indestructible. While Christians have cited these same passages countless times, the perversionist considers our Bible to be a book of fantasy and for them to take us seriously they always insist that we substantiate our passages with science. So let us have some fun and do just that!

The first reason the earth is indestructible is that man simply does not occupy enough space for the planet to be affected by us. People have grave misconceptions that the earth is becoming overcrowded. The truth is that the earth is sparsely populated and offers us a bounty of yet uninhabited, unused land and water. Here is what the numbers say.

- Most estimates agree that the earth contains roughly 510 million square kilometers.[90] Simple unit conversions translate this area into roughly 127 billion acres. Most estimates agree that the earth is 29 percent land and 71 percent sea. This means that we have 37 billion acres of land, and 90 billion acres of sea.

- Most estimates put the current world population at 7.9 billion people.[91]

If we divide the earth's total acreage by the number of people on earth, we find that the earth provides roughly 16 acres of space for every one of us.

Close your eyes and imagine our supposed "crowded earth." Each living person can have 4.64 acres of land and 11.34 acres of water. Now think about this: The earth allows every family of four to occupy 64 acres of earth and not infringe on another human being.

---

90   https://www.universetoday.com/42186/how-big-is-the-earth/.

91   https://www.census.gov/popclock/.

The Perversion of Science

It is absurd to believe that a family of four could in any manner pollute or overconsume the resources provided by 64 acres of planet, yet this is what God has provided to us.

The perversionist will argue that man is not spread out and distributed evenly and that we densely populate cities and create large amounts of pollution. True enough! However, the choice to live in a densely populated area is an individual choice and not one that has anything to do with the occupancy ratio of man to space that the earth offers us.

For sure the concentration of pollution in a densely populated city can be stifling, but that is a parochial situation, and it is not in any way indicative of the overall condition of the earth. The stench and litter on display in these crowded areas is not an indictment that the earth is unable to clean itself, but rather a testament to man's poor decision-making and lack of understanding of the planet. A quick look at New York City will illustrate my point.

New York City occupies 205,000 acres[92] and depending on the source has a population of roughly 8.5 million people.[93] This translates to a woeful population density of only 0.024 acres of space per New York City citizen.

Now imagine what the world looks like through the eyes of the New Yorker who has never lived outside his domain. He sees a city full of litter, homeless people, and crime. He experiences excessively long lines in stores, elbow-to-elbow public transportation, frequent smog-induced air quality warnings and even frequent boil water alerts. Making matters worse, even Central Park, the resident's respite to enjoy open space is becoming overcrowded.[94]

92   https://beef2live.com/story-ranking-states-total-acres-0-108930.
93   https://www.politifact.com/largestcities/.
94   https://assets.centralparknyc.org/pdfs/institute/p2p-up-

If asked to render his opinion on population, pollution, resource availability and the current condition of the earth, this New Yorker, based on his very limited view of the world would likely respond that the planet is in trouble.

Herein lies the root of Satan's ability to convince people that God's Creation is imperfect. It is called myopia, and I am here to tell you that the foundations of every perverted apocalyptic claim, including climate change, renewable energy and diminishing resources are based in this same kind of myopia.

The perversionist focuses on a local set of observations that suit his godless agenda and then projects those findings onto the rest of mankind. I promise you that when these claims of an imperfect world are expanded and forced onto the complete stage of Creation, they crumble as easily as a soda cracker in our clenched fist. So then, let us continue this discussion about the indestructibility of Creation based on the sheer vastness of our planet.

While the New Yorker is packed into his sardine can, the rest of New York State is not so stifled. The State of New York occupies roughly 35 million acres[95] and has a population of roughly 19.5 million people.[96] Applying arithmetic, we come to see that the State of New York offers a comfortable land-to-citizen ratio of 1.79 acres per citizen. While this is still considerably less than the overall earth average of 16 acres per citizen, it ranks as seventy-five times more space per person statewide than the average New York City citizen suffers.

Before leaving our destruction of "the earth is overcrowded" nonsense, I want to have one last bit of fun. The State of Alaska elp/3.002_Report+on+the+Public+Use+of+Central+Park.pdf.
95   https://beef2live.com/story-ranking-states-total-acres-0-108930.
96   https://www.populationu.com/us/new-york-populationz.

occupies 425 million acres,[97] and has a population of roughly 750,000 people.[98] Again, applying arithmetic, we see that Alaska offers a land-to-citizen ratio of 567 acres per citizen. Do you imagine that the average citizen of Alaska feels that the earth is overcrowded and needs man to save it?

My jab here is at the absurdity of overpopulation theory. Even in many of our most crowded cities the ratio of land per person provides the earth a clear, powerful, built-in design advantage to rejuvenate and perpetuate itself. That design has been engineered by none other than our Creator.

Remember also that only a minor portion of mankind qualifies as high consumers of resources. Considering babies, children, elderly, and sedentary individuals, the 16 acres per person gift to us looms as even more impressive.

Let us look now at the other magnificent, infallible, inherent, renewing properties that God has given the earth. Is anyone surprised that these properties are also described in Scripture?

1. Seventy-one percent of earth is water. As we learned earlier, water is a universal solvent.[99] Over time, all compounds, all debris, including dreaded plastics, will unequivocally be reclaimed courtesy of water in our lakes, oceans, and streams. Also, the water in our rains, groundwater and the water dissolved in our air constantly work to return matter to its basic components. The very moment man creates a pollutant, the natural properties of water immediately begin to break it down

---

97   https://beef2live.com/story-ranking-states-total-acres-0-108930.
98   https://www.census.gov/quickfacts/AK.
99   https://www.usgs.gov/special-topics/water-science-school/science/water-universal-solvent#:~:text=Water%20is%20called%20the%20%22universal,every%20living%20thing%20on%20ear.

and reclaim it.

2. Our winds, by simple way of friction, of blowing particles across the earth, have always acted as a natural sandpaper. Regardless of what physical things man creates, earth's winds, over time will file down, and return all of it to the soil as elemental dust. All of it, by God's design, to be used once again by future generations. Whether it is magnificent coliseums, pyramids, forts, bridges or cities, the unstoppable winds of the earth will eventually undo all we have built and reabsorb it. This natural action also applies to chemical compounds, waste, plastics, oil spills and every other product of civilization. This is yet another example of how all matter is conserved.[100]

<u>Ecclesiastes 3:20</u>

All go to one place. All are from the dust, and to dust all return.

3. Since the beginning of recorded history, man has witnessed an awe-inspiring diverse and magnificent array of weather events. Rains that brought multitudes to farm in the Great Plains later turned into drought that drove those multitudes away. Hurricanes, tornadoes, carbon-billowing volcanoes, lightning-driven forest fires, earthquakes, storms, and tsunamis have destroyed more homes, natural habitats, cities, buildings, and trees than any war or pollution.

It should amaze us then that no matter how severe weather events may be, the earth always heals itself by the processes of nature. Much like the new skin that grows over a scraped knee, the earth is constantly renewing and repairing itself.

Most amazing is that once repaired, the sites of destruction become so pristine that men of the next generation would

---

100   https://www.nationalgeographic.org/encyclopedia/wind/.

The Perversion of Science

never know that a past major event occurred.

When the Mount Saint Helens volcano erupted in 1980 it sent fire, lava and poisonous gasses into the atmosphere destroying much of what got into its path. At the time scientists predicted that the destruction was virtually irreversible, and it would take many decades for the area to recover. Yet, in the year 2000 NASA was already reporting a vigorous growth of new vegetation.[101]

And what about the curious case of pavement and concrete? Who among us has not witnessed abandoned infrastructure being overwhelmed and consumed by new, overgrowing vegetation?

Our earth is self-sustaining. That is what God promised.

4. One of my favorite lessons in chemistry class was that of oxidizing agents. In a simplistic description, oxidizing agents are substances/chemicals that "steal" electrons from other elements and compounds.[102]

Like our winds, but in a different manner, oxidizing agents break down host substances and return them to the earth. They are naturally occurring, renewing and protective tools that the earth uses to reclaim itself.

The most powerful, natural oxidizing agents in order of strength are hydrogen, oxygen (ozone) and chlorine. The first two elements are found in bountiful amounts in our atmosphere and are on duty 24-7-365, continually working to renew the earth regardless of our actions.

[101] https://earthobservatory.nasa.gov/images/606/mount-st-helens-rebirth.
[102] https://www.thoughtco.com/definition-of-oxidizing-agent-605459.

Oxygen is always at work reclaiming iron-based substances via the oxidative process of rust, which continues to triumph over supposedly indestructible materials, even stainless steel.

The equation of earth's natural oxidation reclamation of metals is stated below.

$$4Fe + 3O_2 \rightarrow 2Fe_2O_3 \text{ (Fe = iron, O = Oxygen)}$$

Those who believe the earth is running out of resources are confounded by the renewing process of oxidation, but even more so when they realize that it isn't just iron nature reclaims; virtually every metal on earth is subject to being reclaimed by the oxidative process.

Another oxygen-rich compound, carbon dioxide is being portrayed as a pollutant that is destroying the planet. Nothing could be further from the truth. Carbon dioxide is a natural, sustaining gift from God that is created constantly by the very nature of our metabolism.

Carbon dioxide enables plants to manufacture purifying oxygen by way of photosynthesis. Carbon dioxide also stimulates the growth of new vegetation, which in turn produces even more life-sustaining oxygen, and more crops for man to nourish himself with.

The climate change believer strives to reduce our production of carbon dioxide. This is God-hating scientific perversion at its very worst.

Another amazing renewing aspect of earth that we should talk about, and also an oxidizing agent, is ozone. We all know how the atmosphere's natural ozone layer destroys harmful radiation.[103]

103   https://www.news-medical.net/health/What-Are-the-Health-Benefits-of-Protecting-the-Ozone-Layer.aspx.

However, closer to us living on the surface, ozone, especially the temporary mega-doses created by lightning, kills bacteria, fungi, viruses, breaks down carcinogenic hydrocarbons, and destroys the damaging action of radioactive isotopes.

Ozone is one of the reasons why the once radioactive-devastated Hiroshima is today a modern, thriving, healthy, energetic city that rivals the greatest cities in the world. Back in the day, scientists predicted that Hiroshima would be poisoned with radioactivity for centuries. God, however, had other plans.

5. No conversation about the earth's natural ability to clean and sustain itself would be complete without a conversation about rain. In chapter seven we learned the important properties of water. In this conversation the universal solvent and ability to absorb gases are of particular interest.

The ways that rain rejuvenates the earth are innumerable and with each passing day we learn even more. Nonetheless, let us look at some important ways rain contributes to our indestructible planet.

- Falling through the sky rain droplets absorb harmful gasses from the atmosphere, converting them to non-harmful liquids and solutions that can be filtered out in our water treatment systems.[104]

- Via storm drain systems rainwater dissolves harmful chemicals on the ground and then transports them along with dirt and debris to our treatment plants where they can be filtered and returned to the earth as clean water.

- The earth reforests itself and farmer crops feed the world

---
104   https://news.mit.edu/2015/rain-drops-attract-aerosols-clean-air-0828.

thanks to rain.

- Rain creates the ocean currents vital to all aquatic life.
- Rain makes hydroelectric power possible.
- Rain replenishes the water table and constantly maintains the levels of our oceans, lakes, rivers, and streams.
- Perhaps the most impressive benefit provided by rain is that it cools the earth, regulating our temperature. This important feature also completely dismantles the concept of anthropogenic climate change.

<u>Psalm 104:5</u>

He set the earth on its foundations, so that it should never be moved.

The study of the insect world, entomology, sheds another interesting light on man's inability to destroy himself or his planet.

Nowhere in nature is the effect of poison on a population more vicious and aggressive than in the insect world. Each year, millions of dollars are spent on research to find better, safer, and more effective pesticides. Every spring, without exception, we see lawn professionals, city crews, and airplane crop dusters plastering the environment with every manner of insect-killing poison known to mankind.

To our collective dismay, every spring our lawns, gardens and farms are again subject to the same destructive six-legged devils that menaced us the previous season. The expletive-deleted mosquito varmints that stuck us in the neck and sucked out our blood on the golf course last year always seem to send droves of relatives to jolt us again in the new season.

To be sure, the science of why no amount of poison can affect the insect population serves as an eye-opening validation for the Bible's promise of indestructibility. Let us take a closer look at this just how this wonderful phenomenon came to be.

The heavy doses of chemicals kill and maim huge numbers of insects. The initial decline in insect population protects crops, lawns, and flowers, and if the dosing is maintained, the insect population will remain subdued.

However, God's magic happens once the growing season nears its end, and the chemicals are no longer needed. The remaining insects, albeit greatly reduced in number, now face a world in which competition for space, food, water, and breeding partners has also been greatly reduced. Even many of the insect's natural predators will have been diminished.

What science demonstrates to us is that in the absence of strong competition, the surviving insects have a new bounty of food available, and their reproductive energy shifts into overdrive. Before you know it, there are just as many insects living after the insecticide apocalypse as there were before the poisons were administered.

With all our technology, one would believe that man could eradicate all the insects by simply applying more chemicals. But such is not the case. Entomology shows us after a certain level of poison is applied, any additional dose has no effect. How can this be? Again, the laws of Creation always prevail.

First, not all insects will be centered in the main area sprayed. Some of them will be out on the fringes where there is not much competition. Other insects will be in nooks and crannies where the insecticide doesn't reach. Still others may be protected by wind gusts that opportunistically blow the chemical out of harm's way.

More may be protected in nests, and some may have resistance to the chemical applied. Some may simply be far away from where the insecticide is sprayed. Temperature, humidity, and rain can also contribute to the poison not getting to each insect specimen.

Interestingly, as we learned, the second law of thermodynamics explains the phenomenon called entropy.[105] In physics, entropy is often referred to as the law of maximum disorder, and this example of insect survival, it applies beautifully.

Earlier, we dropped a jar of marbles, watched them scatter randomly, then spread out, and eventually come to rest. We know that the marbles will never clump together in a pile. So too, like the marbles, all life forms naturally spread out into what can be called a population resting state. Regardless of the animal population studied, all species, just like marbles in a jar, will spread out to a maximum disorder in which there is no more tendency or urge to expand.

What we see with the insects is the natural force of entropy that causes the population to spread out thereby preventing any single event from destroying it.

Entropy is such a powerful force that even you and I obey its force in our everyday activities. Who among us has not gone to a party or event and walked away from the crowded main room to find some elbow space and fresh air? That is but a simple example of how strongly entropy rules the physical world we live in.

Let us look closer at this business of our resistance. Just as viruses and bacteria develop resistance to drugs, so too do insects develop resistance to pesticides. For forty years a class of chemicals known as pyrethroids was the chemical of choice for killing mosquitoes.

---

[105]   https://www.grc.nasa.gov/www/k-12/airplane/thermo2.html.

Recently, however, mosquitoes are showing resistance to them.[106]

In addition, now we are finding that in many cases the application of mosquito-focused pesticides is increasing the number of mosquitoes. How can this be? Well, the chemicals are killing the mosquitos' natural predators, and as was just explained, a decrease in competition always leads to increased success and growth of a species.[107]

The built-in God-given persistence of species is not just limited to insects, but to all animals. The number of species that were once officially declared extinct that were rediscovered and found to be thriving serves as a constant reminder of just how little science understands about Creation, and how indestructible it is.

In the realm of the ocean alone we have rediscovered twenty-eight species incorrectly identified as extinct.[108] In 2021 alone we discovered ten animals and birds incorrectly labeled as extinct.[109]

The debate over species becoming extinct is one for another book; however, we must consider the framework of this chapter and this discussion. We are speaking about man's inability to destroy God's Creation. Nature taking its course and bringing a species to extinction is something different. That is of God's hand, not ours.

While we are on the topic of resistance, let us not forget that over the years our natural immunity has allowed us to triumph over many diseases and ailments that otherwise would have killed us. Let us also not forget that in God's abundance he has given us the

106   https://www.science.org/content/article/after-40-years-most-important-weapon-against-mosquitoes-may-be-failing.
107   https://www.nationalgeographic.com/environment/article/how-pesticides-actually-increase-mosquito-numbers.
108   https://oceansyrup.com/lazarus-marine-animals/.
109   https://happymag.tv/10-animals-we-thought-were-extinct-but-actually-arent/.

genius of those who develop drugs and therapies, which further make us impervious to extinction.

In the face of overwhelming evidence that God's Creation is indestructible, the perversionist will always pull out what he thinks is his trump card. The nuclear bomb! If I heard it once I heard it a million times:

"But, Tom, we really can destroy the earth! What about nuclear war? There are enough bombs to blow up the earth many times over!"

Yeah, nice try, but again, no cigar! As you might guess, the life cycle and entropy information gleaned from our entomologist friends studying the lives of insect population also applies to man. Like the insects, mankind is simply too widely dispersed for any event to destroy us.

Let it be written, spoken, and etched in stone: there has never been, and there can never be, enough nuclear weapons, regardless of the evil terrorist launching them, to destroy either mankind or the planet.

Like the spraying of insecticide, the potential of spraying nuclear bombs is scientifically modeled in the same manner. Because there are no soldiers, governments, or military threats in most remote parts of the desert, the frozen tundra, the polar caps, mountain tops, or the many millions of acres of uncharted ocean, there are no nuclear warheads pointed at those places. Bombs only get pointed where there are a lot of people, government agencies, financial technology, and military bases.

Another beauty of the blessing of our abundant land is that much of it is remote and uninhabited. In these lands the processes that cleanse, renew, and propagate the earth will be left totally undisturbed, allowed to run full blast.

In addition, there are not enough bombs to blow the world up.[110]

Am I marginalizing the horrors of nuclear war? Of course not, but we must understand that while such a war would kill and injure many as well as poison much of the land, it would not kill and poison enough living things to affect Creation. Man would indeed survive. Everything in life that is, would once again be fruitful in time.

As happens with the insect example, in the nuclear war aftermath there would be less competition for resources, and man would again reproduce and in time repopulate the earth. In addition, the earth would still have all its renewing, sustaining functions and processes left completely intact.

Furthermore, with a reduced population, pollution and resource demand would also be reduced. Accordingly, the earth would repair itself that much quicker.

The takeaway here is that the earth is indestructible. It is unalterable, unchangeable, and governed by its own set of unflappable, built-in protective natural processes. This is not to say that we don't have a moral, ethical, and Christian responsibility to take care of God's gift, because we do. The same Bible that promises an indestructible earth also demands that we be good stewards of it.

Psalm 115:16 ESV

The heavens are the Lord's heavens, but the earth he has given to the children of man.

We have seen through the ages that whatever man has heaped upon the earth, the earth has sneezed, blinked, and then moved along its merry way fixing the damage.

110   https://www.sciencefocus.com/future-technology/what-would-happen-if-all-the-nuclear-bombs-were-detonated/.

The earth will not heat, it will not dry, it will not flood, it will not fail to provide food, minerals, medicines, recreation, plants, animals, rocks, storms, stable weather, or anything else God created for us.

As I seem to keep saying, anyone who thinks or believes the earth is vulnerable is a perversionist of science and an enemy to Christianity and to God. God's earth cannot be destroyed.

Chapter Eleven

Evolution

No book about the science of our existence would be complete without mention of the theory of evolution. I was first exposed academically to Darwin in a college biology class in the winter of 1974. Back in those days evolution was a popular topic, but unlike today, students weren't forced to accept it as fact, and we weren't prevented from challenging it. As a result, many students of my day, myself included, found the theory of evolution to be incredulous. As I learned more, I realized that this concept is blasphemy, it is an attack on God, and it has no scientific support.

Despite countless technological developments and discoveries since Darwin was preaching evolution, there is still not one shred of scientific evidence to support his theory. Even Darwin expressed philosophical doubts about his very own theories,[111] and in a few moments we will shred this perversion.

Genesis 1:20 ESV

And God said, "Let the waters swarm with swarms of living creatures, and let birds fly above the earth across the expanse of the heavens."

Darwin asks us to believe that God did such a lousy job creating man and the animals that as soon as they were given life, they began to metamorphose into other superior life forms to survive.

As ridiculous as this sounds many people believe it to be true. We

[111] https://reasons.org/explore/blogs/blog_channel/darwins-doubt.

Christians must be able to debunk evolutional theory and bring more attention to the Creator.

Darwin wrote that because the metamorphosis of one life form into another would take millions of years to accomplish, most fossil records should display animals that were in a transitional state of evolution. A transitional animal for our reference is one of those theoretical animals that lived in a body that was losing some of its original features while at the same time developing new ones.

As it turns out, not one single fossil has ever been found that shows an animal in such a state of transition. All fossil records show complete animals, and there is no scientific rebuttal to his.

Accordingly, if Darwin was alive today, upon seeing that the fossil records have indeed not supported his predictions of even a single transitional animal, he would himself admit that his theory was bogus.

Darwin's very theoretical transitional animal serves as the death blow to his survival of the fittest beliefs. Let us look closer.

I am sure you have all seen the illustrations of Darwin's fish that gradually experienced its fins transitioning into legs so that after many generations of evolution it could leave the water and walk up onto land. Darwin explained that the reason for this transition was caused by a need to avoid a predator, or to escape a vanishing food supply and find a more bountiful one.

So then, I ask you to picture what would happen as Darwin's fish fins shrunk. First off, it would gradually lose its proficiency as a swimmer, and as a result, water-based predators would find it easier to capture and eat. With a decrease in swimming ability the fish would not evolve; it would pass into extinction because it would not be able to avoid those animals who feed on it. It would never make it up onto land.

But wait, it gets worse for Darwin.

Imagine for a moment that some of these goofy transitional fish did survive and emerged as land animals.

The new legs the animal first developed would be very weak. Evolution, by Darwin's own words takes a long time. Accordingly, there would not have been enough evolutionary time to allow this first-time land dweller to develop speed, power, and agility.

So as the changing fish became easier prey, so too would this newly transitioned land animal be easy prey and the specimens that did make it to land would quickly be eaten and made extinct.

Let us also not forget that the new animals' new lungs, freshly converted from gills, would not have great capacity and the animal would have poor stamina. This "new" animal would be slow and weak and again according to Darwin's survival of the fittest theory this animal would be vulnerable and weak. It would not likely survive.

The reason man has never found fossil evidence of a transitional animal is clear. No such animal ever existed.

I believe that Charles Darwin was not a man of science, but instead a storyteller. I believe he was history's first account of what we know today as a Photoshop artist.

Darwin liked to draw fantastic creatures and if he were a young man today would likely be one of Hollywood's best digital animators. If he were a young man today, he would not gravitate toward biology books, he would instead be mesmerized by the Best Buy salesman showing him the latest computer graphics offerings.

This same logic also applies to nonsensical things like Mayan cave drawings in which insects were portrayed to resemble flying machines. This was not evidence as the pagan insists of the Mayans encountering aliens; it was instead evidence that the idea for the *Transformer* movies and toys was conceived long before modern man commercialized it. I think the Creator of these science-fiction toys and movies should pay a royalty to the Mayans.

God made the animals. Satan made Darwin's army.

Chapter Twelve

Carbon Dating and the Age of Earth

As was the case with chapter 11 and the *theory of evolution,* this is a chapter that could easily be expanded to a library full of volumes and opinions. Fortunately, what needs to be said both scientifically and scripturally can be done in a concise fashion.

The debate on the age of the earth, universe and mankind has separated Christians and non-believers for ages. Christians believe the earth to be a few thousand years old, and non-believers believe it to be billions of years old.

I believe this conversation is a waste of brain energy, for science demonstrates to us that God, the Creator, did indeed make all things. We know that *Genesis 1:1* indeed tells us this, but it is another scriptural passage that speaks to us about the foolish waste of time trying to figure out the age of the earth.

Job 37:5 ESV

God thunders wondrously with his voice; he does great things that we cannot comprehend.

As a man of science, I have never once stopped to ponder the age of earth or mankind, for what value is such knowledge? Regardless of when we were created, God created us. Furthermore, he did it in his time, and he didn't feel it necessary to leave man a handbook to reference his method. Of what good would such instructions be to us? We could never understand it.

I am here to proclaim that whether you are a Christian looking for fortification of our origins, or a pagan looking for historical evidence to prove there is no God, you are wasting your time. You are giving into temptation that is robbing your life of precious time that could be spent on efforts that matter to your fellow man.

Just as the perversions of climate change, the big bang, and renewable energy are beginning to crumble before our very eyes, so, too, will much of the current archaeological/paleontological/geological claims about the age of man and the earth.

Carbon dating has been one of the most popular tools used by perversionists to attack God and Creation. By placing certain objects into an age or time before Bible recognition, this laboratory technique has been a tool to plant seeds of doubt into the minds and hearts of Christians.

As it turns out, much to the dismay of the perversionist, as science has progressed the once accepted results of carbon dating are being shown to be ridiculously inaccurate. To illustrate let us look at what carbon dating is and how it works.

By way of natural processes, radiation passing into our atmosphere collides with and excites a certain amount of naturally abundant nitrogen. This nitrogen, designated as N_{14} is converted by the radiation into a radioactive form of carbon, which is commonly designated C_{14}.[112] This new carbon atom then combines with oxygen to form radioactive carbon dioxide. This radioactive CO_2 makes its way into plants and then by consumption eventually comes to reside in the tissues of both man and animals.

Radioactive C_{14} is physically unstable and over time will discharge its extra energy and eventually come to rest back at its normal and natural C_{12} form. It takes many years for C_{14} to degrade

112   https://www.britannica.com/science/carbon-14-dating.

The Perversion of Science

back to regular C_{12}, and it is by manipulating and examining this somewhat observable physical property that scientists feel they can date certain materials. Scientists use something called chemical half-life to determine the age of objects.

What we know is that the radioactive form of carbon has a half-life of 5,730 years. What this means is that if you were given a pound of C_{14} today, in 5,730 years if you could examine the sample again, you would discover that there would be only one-half pound of C_{14} left, and the other half pound of the sample would be normal C_{12}.

With this assumption at hand, the scientist takes his sample and measures the ratio of the two different carbon types mentioned. He then compares that to what the original concentration was believed to be, and then makes a mathematical calculation of the specimen's age.

In this process the scientist assumes and takes for granted that men and artifacts of all ages, throughout different times and civilizations have all had the same initial identical ratio of C_{14} to C_{12} in their bodies.

This is the first shortcoming of carbon dating, because there is no scientific manner to determine the various carbon concentrations in the body of men and animals that lived tens of thousands of years ago. Diet, weather, location, radiation, general health, and a whole host of other factors influence how much C_{14} any living thing may absorb. To assume that a man living ten thousand years ago experienced the same environment as a man today is, at best, a ridiculous stretch.

The other factor to remember about carbon dating is that after ten half-lives, in other words 57,300 years, the concentration of

C_{14} is below the detection limits of current technology. That said, carbon dating, which is a very sketchy guess to begin with, is only applicable to things 57,300 years or younger.[113]

Recent findings at Cornell University earmark the exact criticisms I have made about the inaccurate assumptions that all things over time shared the same, identical carbon makeup.[114]

The most fascinating new phenomenon regarding carbon dating and the quest to determine the age of Creation comes to us via a newer technology called accelerator mass spectrometry or AMS. AMS is a new, more accurate way to detect and count the amount of C_{14} that exists in a sample or specimen.[115]

Recently, as a celebration to God, and much to the dismay of the perversionist, this new technology has discovered C_{14} on coal samples that are shown to be only forty thousand years old.[116]

You may ask why this is important to Christians. What importance is this to science?

Here is the importance: mainstream archaeologists, geologists and paleontologists have proclaimed by published academic studies that coal was created in the Carboniferous age of civilization some three hundred million years ago.

The implications of finding C_{14} on coal that is only forty thousand years old set aside many years of idiotic research and claims about the prehistoric ages of man and about the supposed significant archaeological digs and discoveries over the years.

---

113 https://www.britannica.com/science/carbon-14-dating.
114 https://www.canadianarchaeology.ca/dating.
115 https://www.radiocarbon.com/accelerator-mass-spectrometry.htm.
116 http://www.talkorigins.org/faqs/c14.html.

The Perversion of Science

The archaeologic discoveries themselves are still wonderous, but our interpretations of how old these things are have now been exposed as irrelevant, inaccurate and totally driven by agenda.

The expansion of AMS could literally end the funding and careers of perversionists across the world. Already carbon dating proponents are scampering to minimize the findings of C_{14} in coal, blaming it on cross-contamination due to bacteria or viruses, the movement of the earth around the coal, and even on errors in measurement. Those who pervert science will do everything possible to marginalize or even hide these kinds of discoveries.

The revelation that the tenets of carbon dating are imploding and that the science of our origin is leaning ever closer to Scripture should surprise nobody. This is just another testament to how, given time, every knee shall bend to God.

Am I saying that I know how old the earth is? Of course not. Remember I am a man of science and a Christian. As such I know not to try and figure out God, and instead be happy to trust what man does not understand. This really keeps my track record of proclamations nice and pristine.

Chapter Thirteen

Sustainability

The concept of sustainability is a well-intended global movement designed to help the earth and mankind meet our needs responsibly today without compromising the ability of future generations to meet their own needs.

To attain this euphoric environmental mindset, sustainability proponents constantly search for technologies and processes that are supposedly environmentally clean and that use what are believed to be renewable resources. These would include minerals, sources of energy, chemicals and materials that are abundant and easily replaced/rejuvenated by the earth.

At face value, sustainability goals seem sensible and the rush of global good feeling we get from jumping on the bandwagon has provided unstoppable momentum for this movement. With that said, many of you are probably wondering why I would mention sustainability in a book focused on exposing perverted science.

As a lifelong Christian and caretaker of God's natural resources, I am here to tell you that the global sustainability movement is indeed perversion. It violates the laws of science, and it is an outright attack on our Lord. It is based in the same Satanic aggression that I have been writing about. That it is cloaked in a blanket of apparent goodwill makes it even more nefarious. God already promised and provided sustainability.

To illuminate my claims about sustainability let us compare what

God's promise of sustainability means versus the modern-day promise of sustainability.

The foundation of those who champion sustainability is a belief that the earth is obliged to allow us to drive cars, fly planes, enjoy a continued parade of new phones games and computers, travel into space, build new cities, casinos, and restaurants, and basically live what we call a modern life while piling on even more new gadgets.

God, however, never made such a guarantee to us. He promised that the earth would always be here for us, and that it will always provide for us. He promised us a home, food and all the necessities to live and enjoy the garden he made for us to dwell in. Again, to highlight, he never mentioned plasma screen televisions or Gucci purses. He never promised Caribbean cruises, all-you-can-eat buffets, or any other lifestyle benefit that we currently enjoy. It is vital to also understand that science also makes no such sustainability promises.

Regardless of which technologies, products and machines man uses, the basic ingredients of our planet are fixed and finite. When God created earth, he blessed it with a given amount of water, minerals, and every other entity both seen and unseen. We cannot make more of these things and we cannot destroy these things.

The nature of earth is that it always changes to suit itself. The earth will sustain us no matter what we do. It will not necessarily sustain our lifestyle. It is our responsibility to live productive, fruitful lives within the conditions that are provided to us while we are alive.

People who indulge in modern sustainability culture are pagans, blasphemers, and knowingly or otherwise haters of God. They promote a fear that one day soon, unless we switch to new ways, we will find ourselves starving, thirsting, immersed in disease and pestilence on a planet that is near destruction.

One of the ways sustainability culture justifies itself is by projecting our demise due to diminishing fossil fuel supplies and the pollution caused by burning them.

However, God didn't directly place fossil fuels on earth. It was the natural properties of earth that produced these wonderful fuels. What God provided was a fixed, indestructible supply of carbon atoms. Just as earth turned dead vegetation and animal remains into oil over time, the earth will again over time turn the byproducts of our civilization into the same fossil fuels, albeit in new locations and concentrations. Dinosaurs or landfills, our planet doesn't care.

That we chose to consume these fuels in a short period of time has no bearing on the earth's sustainability, it has bearing only on our behavior.

The dirty little secret that the perversionist does not share is that the supplies of all our resources are finite. Whatever technology we choose, as the raw materials become more and more tied up into product materials, they will become scarcer in the land and accordingly more costly over time.

These materials will never disappear from earth. Over time, they will all be reabsorbed by the earth and will be ready to be reused again. That, you see, is the true sustainability of Creation. Science gives us the laws of conservation described in our Toolbox chapter, and Scripture reinforces it lest we become unsure of God's promises.

<u>2 Corinthians 5:17</u>

Therefore, if anyone is in Christ, he is a new Creation. The old has passed away; behold, the new has come.

A quick look at the life cycle of fossil fuels demonstrates the impotency of modern-day sustainability goals and highlights the magnificence of Creation.

Imagine for a moment that we do deplete most of our fossil fuels and then imagine also that burning these fuels really does pollute the earth and warm the climate. What happens next?

Well, as we depleted fossil fuels, they would become more expensive, perhaps even cost-prohibitive. As a result of this man would begin using less fossil fuel. Accordingly, the use of less fossil fuel would create less pollution and therefore less global warming. This in turn would allow the earth to clean itself faster than ever.

So, am I saying the best way to find cleaner energy and reduce pollution is to keep using the resources we already have? Of course, that is exactly what I am saying. This is what God and science have always told us to do.

We have all heard the euphemism "necessity is the mother of invention," but this isn't really a euphemism; it is a promise from God.

Over and over, he tells us to fear not, and he assures us he will provide. But as I have mentioned before, the resources that he provides to us go far beyond things we can see and touch. He provides us innovation, creativity, problem-solving and every future solution we need as the earth goes through its changes.

It is God who invented sustainability, and it is he who has provided for it.

Exodus 35:31–31

And he has filled him with the Spirit of God, with skill, with intelligence, with knowledge, and with all craftsmanship, to devise artistic designs, to work in gold and silver and bronze.

Throughout time the greatest discoveries and invention were born naturally by man using the gifts of his skills, creativity and drive to make things better. There was no government mandate or social movement that caused Edison, the Wright brothers, Salk, Guttenberg, Benz, Bell, Jenner (vaccine in 1796), or many others to dream up and create their new life-enhancing, sustaining inventions.

There were no mandates or programs in place to force the development of the wheel, the lever, fire, the hammer, or the fishing net.

All these things, and more, came to man from the Spirit of God. Sustainability is not a social campaign. It is part of God's promise, and we don't have to lift a finger to see it unfold over and over, right before our very eyes.

In closing this chapter, I will again be very clear. Any man who purveys the concept of saving the planet, of developing sustainable technology to allow man to survive is misguided. He is antithetical to our faith, and he is the swine we are warned not to cast pearls before.

Our future is guaranteed. It has been provided for. Any moment spent trying to take responsibility for sustaining man is an act that pleases Satan and draws us away from God. It is blasphemy.

We are already good people. We are born with the nature to make things better for each other. Fear not, for whatever form our future takes, it will be of God, it will be of nature, and we will flourish in it.

<u>Matthew 6:34</u>

Therefore, do not be anxious about tomorrow, for tomorrow will be

The Perversion of Science

anxious for itself. Sufficient for the day is its own trouble.

Chapter Fourteen

Parting Thoughts

Writing this book has been a cathartic experience for me. Four times it was finished, and four times I scrapped the entire work to begin again. With each of those four efforts, despite my passion for spreading the word about real science, the book wound up floundering and not expressing what I felt was burning inside of me.

The more I exposed the perversions of science, the less fulfilled I felt. I always believed that apocalyptic scientific prognostications were contrary to God's teachings but in the beginning of my journey I thought that my process should be to first write a purely secular book and then follow it up with another book more catered to Christians.

The reason unhappiness caused me to shred the first four attempts at this book is what I call the Peter Syndrome. Three times Peter denied knowing Jesus and it changed him forever.

In my work, at the levels of CEOs, investors, academics, and politicians, there are very few Christians. From the time I rose from being a sales engineer for major corporations, to starting my own corporation and taking the position of an industry leader, I have often been a fish out of water.

I cannot tell you how many times I sat in meetings listening to, and holding my tongue about, God's promises while colleagues spoke self-assuredly that all these foolish concepts of climate, sustainability and green energy were real.

The reason I held my tongue of course was that speaking the truth might have upset a potential investor, boss or client who believed in these things. Even worse, the mere mention of God in a business conversation would have earmarked me as a weirdo to most.

On one occasion a then-partner stormed into my office angry that my writing an article against climate change on my blog caused us to lose a lucrative research grant. I am ashamed to admit that I quickly pulled the article.

So you see, in my own way, like Peter, I too, on multiple occasions, denied Jesus for fear of repercussions. Every time I went along with such perverted topics, simply to further my company or my career I again denied God. I will also tell you that when I went along with such an agenda, I felt sick to my stomach afterward.

Some may find my feelings to be a stretch, but I don't.

As I look around the world each day, I see in people more and more frantic fear coupled with confusion, indecision, wasting of precious time, opportunity, and resources. All of this at the hands of Satan and people who without the foundation of God have become soldiers of his war on Creation. We bite our tongues and hold back what is right for fear of personal repercussions. The pressure to be politically correct and not offend others grows with each passing moment.

So, this book is my reconciling, my line in the sand where I say, "No more." Peter was called to his tasks, and answered them magnificently after Jesus left this world. Other than identifying with Peter's weak moments, I boast no similarity or shared nobility with him. But I have learned from him.

Perhaps like the sword he drew in the Garden of Gethsemane, my book is my sword? I don't know and I must be vigilant for my passion for science and God quickly rises my anger against those who attack it. However, I will pray for the Holy Spirit to keep me calm, strong, and focused on helping others to recognize how identical God's promises are to the promises of science.

Sadly, most of those I refer to as perversionists, will never open their minds and hearts to God. As such you can be sure that my book will serve as a gauntlet that will bring me criticism, ridicule, and personal attacks.

I am ready for this because I know I am in good company. The right company.

John 15:20 ESV

Remember the word that I said to you: "A servant is not greater than his master." If they persecuted me, they will also persecute you. If they kept my word, they will also keep yours.

2 Timothy 3:12 ESV

Indeed, all who desire to live a godly life in Christ Jesus will be persecuted.

THE END

About the Author

Of my worldly loves, science and mathematics have always ranked high. As a boy, I studied the constellations, launched model rockets, built electronics to alter the sound of my guitar, and even blew up a few things with homemade concoctions. I have always been fascinated to learn how and why things work.

In high school, I studied subjects like chemistry, biology, and algebra. In college, I moved on to more advanced disciplines such as organic chemistry, molecular cellular biology, calculus and physics, leading to a Bachelor of Science degree from Youngstown State University in biology with a chemistry minor. I have been blessed with a career that not only has depended on these scientific foundations but has afforded me the daily opportunity to observe just how flawlessly those precious laws and principles are proven in every aspect of our lives.

My first job out of college was as a phlebotomist where I learned sterile technique, blood serum collecting, and some basic analytical laboratory procedures. I quickly progressed to hospital-based hemodialysis units where I was trained to perform patient assessments, calculate treatment parameters, insert needles, and administer countless hemodialysis treatments. Along the journey, I was promoted, trained, and given the responsibilities of maintenance and calibration of dialysis machines and water purification systems with an additional call to review and test new health-care products.

Around 1983, I was hired by a regional company that designed water purification technology for industry. I first served as a specialist providing solutions to the health-care, pharmaceutical, analytical/

laboratory and biotech industries. Over time, these responsibilities grew into the industrial arena where I helped industries not only purify water for process, but also recover precious materials, minimize, and clean waste streams, improve efficiency, and reduce energy consumption.

The broad spectrum of industries that looked to me for help presented a constantly changing scientific challenge. I helped companies in the automotive, power-generating, metal finishing, electronics/circuit board, food, pharmaceutical, beverage, chemical, aerospace, and other industries. Over the years, my work demanded that I become an integral partner in my customer's process.

In 1998, I took an unusual career sidestep to build and operate a commercial recording studio and run my own business. Much to my surprise, while I was enjoying the self-indulgent passion of composing and promoting my own music, my understanding of physics and acoustics allowed me to develop a production reputation that attracted some famous artists and composers as customers, and found me performing my own music on national network television.

Success in the music industry led me to write numerous magazine articles and author a book (*Make Money With Your Studio*, Hal Leonard). I garnered speaking invitations at some of the finest music technology schools and professional conventions in America. My understanding of the physics and engineering of sound provided me with yet another wonderful platform to behold God's magnificent science and blessings.

In 2002, I felt God's call of science. I reentered the world of environmental technology and took a position designing and implementing water purification, resource recovery, and environmental compliance processes.

The Perversion of Science

While I am not a science professor or researcher, I do have one decided and impressive advantage over most public figures and professors speaking on these issues today: I have lived everything that I share. There is absolutely nothing theoretical or conjectural in my words. There is no guesswork, no supposition, and no credible critique against any of the scientific principles that follow. Whether it is in the laboratory, the ocean, desert, outer space, or the church, the tools provided in this book cannot be contradicted.

From a spiritual side, I was raised Roman Catholic and always had a desire to know and understand God. Over the years, regardless of where life took me, I would somehow always wind up in the company and fellowship of Christians.

Around 1990, I began to open more to Scripture and move away from some of the doctrines of organized religion. Thanks to three very important men in my life, Pastor Bill Watson, Pastor Rusty Wills, and my current pastor and bowling nemesis, Pastor Jack Hollis, I have come to understand how nothing in the world of man is new, contradictory, or perplexing to God.

I also give thanks to my mother, Mary, and father, Charles. As a result of my life with them I cannot remember a time in my life when I did not know God and his Son, Jesus Christ.

Throughout my career, more times than I can tell you, I would learn new things about earth and science and then stand in awe at how emphatically Scripture supported the science I was practicing and the observations I was making.

I wrote this book first to celebrate the beautiful relationship between the Creator and the science we rely on so much, and secondly to expose as frauds those who dare to suggest that our planet cannot thrive without man's help.

I believe that my credentials more than qualify me as a credible expert on the perversion of science and its attack on God. While I am at the same time humbled and proud of all I have learned, there is a thunderous, godly force beyond my curriculum vitae that has spurred me forward.

When I was young, if I had my way, a career in science and environmental technology would not have been my choice. Out of college, I preferred playing rock-n-roll, chasing girls, and sleeping until three o'clock in the afternoon as opposed to studying Avogadro. If left to my own devices, I think that I would have grown up to be a buffoon.

Over the years there were times when I tried to veer away from my science career into something more glamorous, like music. However, fate, or so I thought, always presented new opportunities, and drew me back into the environmental sciences.

Although I've excelled in the jobs I've held, the industrial world at times left me frustrated. My passion for science and mathematics was always present, but the administrative quagmires and corporate politics were hurdles that many times, for reasons I didn't always understand, made me restless and unhappy.

There were times I prayed and asked God to get me out of the environmental industry and into something that I thought would be more fun. When I opened my recording studio in 1998, I was pretty sure that God answered my prayers and gave me the vocational freedom that I so heartily desired. But even my dream job ran its course, and within a time frame that seemed like a blink of an eye, I was again working in the environmental field.

In 2003, I finally accepted without question that it was God's will for me to remain immersed in the vocation of environmental sciences and that no amount of effort on my part was going to break that will. I can honestly say that all my efforts to leave my vocation left me feeling like Bill Murray's character in the movie *Groundhog Day*.

It was in that year that I began to view the environmental industry as my Ark. Unlike Noah, God didn't tell me what I was building or why. I did believe that when the time was right, he would reveal the plan that he had prepared for me.

I know now that my work is my calling, and I see that God has nurtured and prepared me with the knowledge and experience to combat those who pervert science. Inspired by the fire of the Holy Spirit, I stand ready to defend God and his Creation against any attack that the perversionists cast our way.

www.ingramcontent.com/pod-product-compliance
Lightning Source LLC
Chambersburg PA
CBHW070647160426
43194CB00009B/1608